Discovering KHAO LAK

For Tourists, Individual Travellers and Families

R. Kobi

Impressum

Text: Copyright © 2016 by Rudolf Kobi
Unter Brieschhalden 24
CH-4132 Muttenz
Switzerland
Ruco.kobi@gmail.com
All rights reserved
Edition 1 July 2016

The content of this book may not be copied without permission of the author. A transfer or resale of the book is not permitted without written permission of the author.
Disclaimer: The contents have been carefully researched or derive from personal experience of the author. However, the author is not liable for consequences of errors, which the text could be flawed with.
All pictures by C. Kobi
Translated from 'Khao Lak Entdecken' by C. Kobi
English proofreading by S. Woodtli (all remaining mistakes are my own.)
Map images created with ShareMap.org
Coordinates with the kind help of R. Fackler

ISBN: 1534930019
ISBN−13: 978-1534930018

Table Of Contents

Authors Note 7
About Khao Lak 9
Getting Around in Khao Lak 16
Hotels in Khao Lak 21
Food in Khao Lak / Restaurants 22
Nightlife in Khao Lak 25
Markets and shopping 27
Waterfalls 29
Lam Ru National Park 38
Kapong and Hot Springs 39
Takua Pa Old Town 41
Orchid Garden und Butterfly Farm Khao Lak 43
Khao Lak Minigolf 44
Khao Lak Turtle Sanctuary 45
Temples and Religion 47
Phang Nga 54
Phung Chan Cave 55
Sa Nang Manora Waterfall Forest Park 55
Phang Nga Bay Tour 56
Phang Nga Bay on a Chinese Junk 60
Tsunami 2004 Museum, Boat and Memorial 61

Ko Kho Khao	65
Dive- und Snorkel-Tours	66
Similan Islands	67
Koh Tachai	70
Surin Islands	71
Takua Pa Mangroves – „little Amazon"	72
Bamboo Rafting	73
Attractions with Elephants	74
Khao Sok National Park	77
Kayaking (or Bamboo-Rafting) on the Sok River	80
Cheow Lan Lake	81
Massage	85
At the Tailor	87
Phuket	89
Sarasin Bridge	90
Phuket Waterpark – Splash Jungle	91
North-east Phuket	91
Bang Rong Pier	94
Phuket Gibbon Rehabilitation Project und Bang Pae Waterfall	95
Heroines Monument	97
Phuket Town	98
Phuket Aquarium	99
Wat Chalong	99

Promthep Cape	101
Karon (Kata) Viewpoint: 3-Beaches Viewpoint	102
Patong Zorbing	103
More Things	104
To Do and See On Phuket	104
Overview Map	106
What For Who? Tips For Everyone	107
Do's and Don'ts in Thailand	109
Eating in Thailand	110
Toilets	113
Electricity	114
Telephone, Roaming, Internet	115
Withdrawing Money	117
Health	118
Traffic In Thailand: A Survival Guide	125
In Case Of A Traffic Accident	129
Thai for Tourists	130

Authors Note

Thailand is – and rightly so – a popular tourist destination. It has a lot to offer for everyone, from backpackers to tourists to families. There is everything from fine dining to clean beaches, fantastic landscapes to pleasant weather and cultural places. You could say that it is the ideal holiday destination.

There are some guides to Thailand – for the south and for the popular Phuket ... but Khao Lak is mentioned (if at all) only as a side note in most. A real deficit.

So here is a guide covering Khao Lak and the surrounding area, which will put an end to this. In this guide you will find about 60 attractions and tips just for Khao Lak and the immediate vicinity.

On what kind of a basis did I write this guide? I have been visiting this wonderful country almost yearly for over 20 years. In the last years we were mainly in Phuket and Khao Lak. While I was initially traveling alone, I now travel with my family – and a child. So there will be tips for traveling with family / children – but not so many for backpackers.

In the book, I cover offered tours as well as self-drive trips and excursions. I will not advise you on a special tour provider because many of them offer the same or at least similar tours. The same applies to restaurants (with one exception).

The appendix contains useful general information for the visit to Thailand and a list of do's and don'ts, typical dishes as well as some Thai language for tourists.

I hope this guide proves useful in practical use.

Because it is a work in progress – and can be expanded and/or changed, I look forward to your feedback and suggestions at ruco.kobi@gmail.com

Many greetings and happy holidays wishes

Ruedi

About Khao Lak

Khao Lak is not *one* place, but rather **a series of small towns** in the Takua Pa district of the Phang Nga Province in southern Thailand.

Today Khao Lak lives off tourism. But compared to Phuket it's not nearly as overrun by mass tourism and it still retains its Thai charm in many places and has a lot of places yet to be discovered.

The name "Khao Lak" means "Mountain Lak", which is the main elevation in the otherwise rather hilly region. But even this "mountain" only has a height of 1050 meters. It is located in the Khao Lak Lam Ru National Park.

There are 7 national parks (those at sea included) within an area of 70 km around Khao Lak. The coast with its golden sandy beaches belongs to the most beautiful ones in Thailand. In the hinterland there are rainforest-covered hills. There are Mangrove forests close by and rocky steep hills with incredibly spectacular views. Off the coast there are the coral reefs of the Similan and Surin islands where you can dive with turtles and manta rays.

Khao Lak is renowned for its quiet atmosphere and is the starting point for diving and snorkeling trips to the Similan and Surin Islands. It differs from Phuket with its quiet hotels of higher class, less overcrowded beaches, family-friendly nightlife and a local building code that prohibits the construction of buildings higher than a coconut palm tree ... so Khao Lak only grows horizontally, not vertically.

Climate

Khao Lak is influenced by two monsoons that occur seasonally: the southwest monsoon and the northeast monsoon. The southwest monsoon begins in April, when a current brings warm and moist air and thus rain from the Indian Ocean. It ends in October, which is the wettest month in Khao Lak. The following months are under the influence of northeast winds from China and are much drier. Therefore, the time from November to March is considered the dry season. March is the hottest month.

From a tourist point of view, the dry season (between October and May), is perfect to visit Khao Lak. But even on a "rainy day" it is not bad at all. It usually rains in the late afternoon or early evening and even then often just briefly. The rain can also only occur very locally – which falsifies the statistics, so the indication of the number of rainy days is misleading.

Climate table

	Jan	Feb	Mar	Apr	May	Jun	Jul	Aug	Sept	Okt	Nov	Dez
Maximal-temp (°C)	33	34	35	34	33	32	32	31	31	32	31	31
Minimal-temp (°C)	21	22	23	24	24	24	24	24	23	23	23	22
Precipitation (mm)	33	36	68	205	527	406	452	478	582	476	250	48
rainy days	4	4	7	15	24	23	21	23	24	22	16	6

How to get there

Khao Lak is located about 80 km **north of Phuket** and you would usually reach it after arriving at Phuket airport and a one hour transfer via the **Sarasin Bridge** on Route 4 – one of the main routes through Thailand.

Of course there is also public transport: public buses operate between Phuket and Khao Lak. Most visitors, however, are picked up by the hotel's own bus or minivan, or transfer via taxi. Transfer by taxi is about 1500 baht for one way.

At the airport you can rent cars from the major rental agencies. The way to Khao Lak by car is easy: from the airport you take the road 402 north (away from of Phuket). Then you always keep left if the road divides (along the coast) – except for the one fork in the village of Thai Mueang ... there you have to take the road to the right, even if it looks as if you should go straight – if you miss this, you end up in a dead end on the beach road.

Once you have crossed a hill over curvy roads you are in Bang La On – the real heart of Khao Lak region.

Khao Lak itself lies along the **road No. 4**,. It is called Phetkasem Road here. The villages lie between the coast and the wooded backcountry.

Beaches and places

(From south to the north)

Khao Lak Beach – This is the most southern beach, located in front of the Hill Lak, over which the road travels. The beach is 700 m long, embedded between the Lam Ru National Park on the right side and flat rocks on the left side.

Nang Thong Beach – in Bang La On – often (falsely) called Khao Lak, is the "center" of the Khao Lak region. It is also the most touristy place with most restaurants and shops (tailors, art galleries and of course diving centers ...). The further north or south you go, the less touristy and more "Thai" it gets.
It's an approximately 2.5 km long beach divided by long rocks overgrown with mussels, which protrude up to 45 meters into the Andaman Sea. The rock formation Nag Thong (Golden Lady) gave the beach its name. During the monsoon season you cannot swim here because of the waves. In the north, the beach is bordered by the Bang Niang River, which you can wade through at low tide.

Bang Niang Beach – in the village of the same name, 2-3 km north of Bang La On. This is the place with the most bars and nightlife and the daily market.
The beach here is largely rock-free and thanks to the coral reef in front of it, swimming is almost always possible, even during the monsoon season, when the waves are higher.

Khuk Khak Beach – in the village of the same name, 2-3 km north of Bang Niang. The village is the administrative headquarter and there are small shops, the post office, a police station and a gas station. The sandy beach is a shallow drop, about 8 km long and is divided by two rivers. On the south it borders Cape Coral (a landscape projection into the sea).

Laem Pakarang (Coral Cape) is a beach with fine sand. The bay is again divided by some large rocks protruding into the sea. You should wear slippers here because of the pieces of coral in the sand – and because there are stingrays. At low tide, an impressive coral reef table is visible.

Bang Sak is a gently curved and sloping sandy beach with pieces of coral in the sand.

All these beaches are public (like all beaches in Thailand). The hotels have their infrastructure like parasols and deckchairs, but the beach strip is mostly free of them and open for everyone.

Orientation in Khao Lak

If you say "Khao Lak" you could mean any of these beaches – even if they extend over a total of 25 km along the coast. This sometimes makes it difficult to communicate where to meet. One needs more precise directions: Which beach? Which town? Near the sea? Located off the Highway 4?

Even the (hotel) addresses are not very meaningful. Somehow, all of them have Phangnga and Moo something in it, and oddly enough most Khuk Khak – even if Khuk Khak is at the further end, on Nang Thong Beach. This is probably because the county administration is there.

For this reason, I do not use the postal addresses of the attractions here, but rather the descriptions to get there and in addition to that the coordinates in decimal degrees (provided by Google) and in GMS (in degrees, minutes, seconds). You can use them for your satnav.

Type	Latitude	Longitude
DG	8.65112	98.25252
GMS	N 8° 39' 4.032"	O 98° 15' 9.072"

Map of beaches / Villages Khao Lak

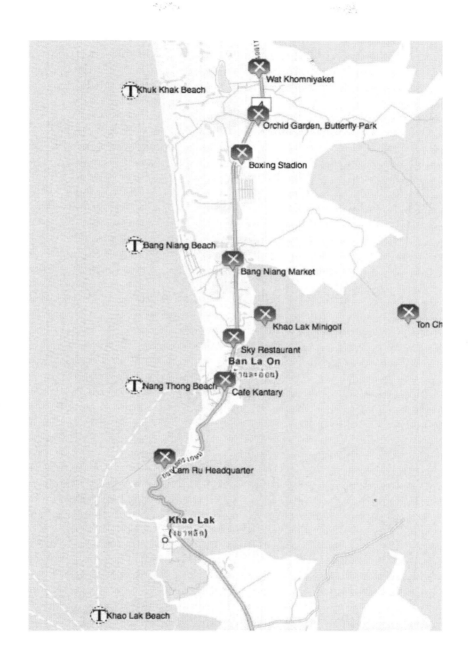

Getting Around in Khao Lak

Pedestrians

As a pedestrian you may encounter some problems in Thailand – and Khao Lak is no exception here. Many sidewalks are in poor condition, so you have to be alert to avoid holes, (semi-) open sewer lids or loose and protruding stones. Electricity pylons, signal masts and other things may be mounted right in the middle of the sidewalk. The walkway edges vary in height and are often considerably higher than in Europe.

So concentration is called for if walking here and – if you have a stroller – it is even a bit more strenuous, but still feasible .

Crossing the street can be adventurous. For us, the cars approach from the wrong side (from the right) and pedestrian crossings (zebra crossings) often serve more as decoration – only a minority of drivers will stop to let a pedestrian cross.

Taxis / Tuk Tuks / guided Tours

Those who do not rent a car – because they do not dare or feel like driving here or – but want to explore Khao Lak and the surrounding area, depend on private taxi drivers or tours.

Although prices went up in the past 15 years, they are still moderate enough that one can well afford it. Taxis are a little more expensive here in the South than in Bangkok ... but they do not drag you from gift shop to gift shop or try to change the desired destination with statements like "temple closed today" (which by the way is never true). The taxi drivers here are numerous and friendly and not very intrusive ... a simple shake of the head is enough when you are asked if you need a taxi. In front of the big hotels, there is normally a taxi rank, even (or especially) if the hotel is quite isolated.

Most drivers have fixed prices in their heads for frequent destinations and routes such as airport transfers (about 1500 Baht) or to the market in Bang Niang (300 baht for up to 4 persons).

For longer trips, there are 2 pricing models that you can arrange with the drivers:

Hourly Rate: for example 2000 baht for 4 hours, then 500 baht per hour – depending on the distance.

Fixed price for the whole trip: for example, 2500 Baht for the 3 Temple Tour.

Keep in mind that in pre-existing tours often include eating and a (English or German-speaking) guide in the quoted price.

Renting a vehicle

I recommend doing that if you want to be truly flexible and independent and if you dare driving the Thai roads (and thus on the left). Motorcycles, scooters and cars can be rented without difficulties at many places in Khao Lak. Those who book from home can get their car at the airport and drive up to Khao Lak by themselves without having to rely on being picked up by a hotel (shuttle) bus.

Cars

Several international car rental companies have rental stations in Phuket; *Hertz* and *Budget* in Khao Lak itself (near the police boat), also worth mentioning is *Thai Rent a Car* in Khao Lak.

Especially in high season it may well be that cars are not available on short notice or have to be brought up from Phuket – therefore it is sometimes cheaper to rent them prior to arrival or down in Phuket.

I would caution you not to rent a car on the roadside, as they are privately rented cars – and thus not insured

Scooters / mopeds

Scooters can be rented in the tourist resorts in many places, sometimes at the hotel itself.

Prices vary depending on location and length of rental – the longer the time, the cheaper the rent is usually. Daily rates are about 150 to 250 baht.

Petrol is sold at filling stations and on the roadside – the bottles with the red content on the wooden racks. The price is about 40 baht per liter – and therefore slightly more expensive than at the station and the quality is not the same.

Bikes / Bicycles

Biking provides you with a better insight into the country and local life than driving a car, but it is more strenuous in the heat. However, there are actually bicycle paths in Khao Lak now.

Many hotels offer rental bikes as a good way to explore the area because Khao Lak and the whole stretch along the coast is mostly flat. The hinterland is hilly and in the south there is the "mountain" Lak. Where are hills are, there is also forest. Do not go off-road through the forest: there are often snakes there, so even Thais do not just trudge or bike through the bushes. However crossing the forest on the roads is safe.

Those who do not yet know what to go and see, can book one of the guided bike tours, which visits various points of interest: waterfalls, villages, beaches. Some are combined with kayak trips or bathing in a river.

Tips for renting a vehicle:

If you rent a motor vehicle in Thailand you now need an international drivers license. Even if the rental company does not always check the validity of the license, this could be a problem with police controls or insurance later.

Occasionally, the deposit of a passport is required for the rent (also with motorcycles). This should not be done in any case. On the one hand because you may need to present it upon police checks and on the other hand because the rental agency could really cause you problems in the event of damage – you need it for your departure. It is better if the rental agency requires a cash deposit or deposit via credit card. Sometimes also a copy of the passport will do.

Insurance of the car will cover damage to person and vehicle, but usually only with an excess of up to 50'000 baht.

Check vehicles for damage before you leave the station and have them written down – otherwise you may have to pay for repairs later. If you take a digital photo with a timestamp, this may help later in the case of possible claims.

Insurance for mopeds only covers personal injury, not vehicle damage, which you have to pay yourself. At least the repairs here are often way cheaper than at home.

Note the number of the insurer and let the rental company give you a phone number which you can contact in case of an accident.

More tips on road traffic and the procedure in case of an accident can be found in the appendix.

Road through Thai Muang

Hotels in Khao Lak

Hotels and accommodation in Khao Lak are plenty and there is something for every budget: from backpacker hostels to luxury hotels.

In general, they still focus less on mass tourism here than below in Phuket, but of course you can also get super-cheap deals or just stay all inclusive where you never (have to) leave the hotel area.

It is up your to the personal preferences and budget which hotel you choose – and where in Khao Lak. If you want nightlife, I recommend the area around Bang Niang. If you want to stay close to many restaurants and shops and will be mainly on foot, then choose Nang Thong. Some exclusive resorts are located further north ... beyond walking distance from the busy villages, but they also have some restaurants and small shops close by.

The beaches are nice, wherever you stay in Khao Lak.

Food in Khao Lak / Restaurants

There are many restaurants in Khao Lak, from small local joints to luxury restaurants with continental food – there even is a McDonalds, if you should need that. There are countless recommendations on the internet for the restaurants. One travel site even wrote that they have received as many recommendations just for Khao Lak as for the rest of Thailand. Why? The food is good in just about any restaurant, but what stands out in Khao Lak is the wonderful friendly service, which ensures that customers return. Often, you get to be friends with the staff.

Restaurant Sky

That was not different with us – although we have initially tried many restaurants, we ended with Jin. At the time, she was working in the Phulay Bar and Restaurant, at the very southern end of Bang La On (before the hill). She not only cooks fantastically, but also treated our little boy so great. Three years ago, she opened her own restaurant, The Sky. The menu is fantastically varied – and yet she manages to cook everything freshly and to listen to the wishes of the guests – so that the meals are customized from Thai "hot-spicy" to "not so spicy, please" (read: edible for tourists). I highly recommend the Tempura (vegetables and shrimps fried in batter) and of course the Tom Kha Gai soup. (More about Thai food can be found at the end of the Guide.)

The Sky Restaurant in Khao Lak is definitely worth a visit (and more) – and if you are there, say "Hi" to Jin by the Kobis!

Location: Between La On and Bang Niang, next to the road leading to the Lah Own Resort. Parking is possible (beyond the bike lane).
DG: 8.65112, 98.25252
GMS: N 8°39'4.032" O 98°15'9.072"

I will let you discover the rest of the restaurants on your own – that is some of the real fun here because you can eat well almost anywhere and also find something for every budget.

On the market in Bang Niang there are many food stalls (as usual in Thailand) – something for the more adventurous to try.

Cafe Kantary

For those who would like to eat a Black Forest cake like at home, have a real ice-cream or have a craving for an iced coffee, I warmly recommend the Café Kantary. In the stylish-white interior you can enjoy a variety of cakes, waffles, pancakes, ice-cream or frappés .

Location: Ban La On (the "center" of Khao Lak) on the main road, (sea side), just south of the McDonalds.
DG 8.64255 98.25077
GMS   N 8° 38' 33.18"   O 98° 15' 2.772"

Private Dinner at the beach

This is romance pure. Because of the location of Khao Lak at the west coast you have many places to eat with a view of the sunset – mainly those located on the beach. But if you want something very special, check out if your hotel offers private dinners on the beach. There is little that is more romantic than a fine meal at sunset, with rustling waves and your feet in the sand. And ... it is often less pricey than you may expect. It is about as much as a meal in a good restaurant at home – without all these extras you have here.

Dinner and Sunset

Nightlife in Khao Lak

Khao Lak has not earned its reputation as a family destination unjustly. Those looking for excitement and party life, can find more of this further south in Phuket (namely Patong) or on Pattaya.

But even here you can find friendly bars and small clubs with live music that are open after 11 pm and serve alcohol and snacks. Especially in high season you can find your place here:

In Bang Niang, at the Jerung Street: Bebob Bar, Smile Bar – often with entertainers.
With a band of up to five musicians: the most famous / biggest is the Zantika Nightclub, but there is also the 12 Bar, Degree Bar, Song's Bar and the Bangrak Bar – right next to the 7/11.

In Nang Tong: Happy Snapper Bar – for some, this is the best in Khao Lak, with pretty decoration, changing events and live bands starting from 10 pm. People begin to dance around midnight.

In La On: MonkeyBar with reggae music, Running Deer, Tarzan Bar.

It is striking that most of the bars are situated on the road inland. The reason for this is that all the buildings located on the beach were destroyed in the 2004 tsunami and the owners were therefore reluctant to build there again. That has only changed in recent years, so that there are beach bars again, but usually they are smaller. Some of them, like the Thai Bar, organize Full Moon Parties in high season once a month.

Cocktails usually cost around 120 baht, beer between 60 and 90 baht.

Moo Moo's Cabaret

This is Khao Laks response to the **Simon Cabaret** in Phuket and shows a colorful and loud ladyboy show with performances from 9.45 pm to 11:15 pm every night. For those who do not know yet: the term "ladyboy" refers to a very elegantly dressed and feminine looking transgender in Thailand.

The cabaret can be found just south of the Bang Niang market next to the bridge. Entrance is free, but the drinks and cocktails are slightly more expensive. Directly opposite there is the **"Ladyboy Cabaret"**, which starts earlier with a similar show .

Khao Lak Boxing Stadium

Thai boxing is a popular sport in Thailand and the participants train long and hard for it. Some stadiums in very touristy areas such as Patong present audiences with staged fights, but others take it very seriously. Khao Lak Boxing Stadium is the true thing and has weekly fights taking place. The prices to be won are high, there is betting and the mood is good.

The fights are advertised by driving up and down the road in Khao Lak and the surrounding area with (loud) speaker-cars and giant posters: "Tonight, and Tonight Only ... !"

Fights take place every Friday night, starting at 9.45 pm

Location: Opposite the 7-Eleven / gas station on Highway 4 quite north.

DG 8.68876 98.25389
GMS   N 8° 41' 19.536" O 98° 15' 14.003"

Markets and shopping

In Thai life markets play a major role: this is the place where you shop for food or go eating if you do not have a kitchen, which however seems to be more common in northern Thailand. So the markets in and around Khao Lak are not exclusively a tourist thing.

In Bang Niang there is **a permanent market** – opposite of the police boat. Monday, Wednesday and Saturday afternoon are its main times – on Saturday the market is the largest.

To protect against the sun you are shopping under suspended roofs, towels, umbrellas and tent roofs. One can find everything needed for daily life: fruit, vegetables, meat, fish, spices, clothes, shoes, watches, flowers and all kinds of souvenirs.

There are a lot of food stalls selling all kinds of snacks, such as chicken wings, sticky rice, Padthai, meat skewers and more. Particularly bold tourists can have a try at the fried beetles (which are not so bad; they are very crispy, and with a little salt they are in fact edible.

In addition to the market, there are a few small restaurants and bars next to it where you can sit and watch the market life for a while.

DG 8.66696 98.25245
GMS   N 8° 40' 1.056"   O 98° 15' 8.819"

In Khuk Khak, approximately 3 km north of Bang Niang, is a market at the bus station. It is open daily from early morning until about noon. The locals (and the restaurant operators) buy their fresh vegetables, fruits, fish and meat here.

In Takua Pa, there is also a large daily market. It is best to ask a local for directions if you cannot find it.

In addition to these daily markets there is a **market in the Old Town of Takua Pa on Sundays**, which is now also visited by tourist trips (see Old Town Tip further down).

For other things to buy go to the **7-Eleven supermarkets**. There are a few of them in Khao Lak and the surrounding area.

Western products can be found in the **Nang Thong supermarket**. It is located on the corner of Road Nr. 4 (the main street) and the road that leads to the Nang Thong beach. You will also find a wide range of wines there.

Alcoholic beverages are not as easy to be found in stores in Thailand ... and obviously there are now restrictions, so you cannot purchase alcoholic beverages at all times. (Although that is not followed equally strict everywhere). It is allowed to buy alcohol between 11 am to 2 pm and from 5 pm to midnight. On election days or religious holidays you may not be able to buy alcohol anywhere. In restaurants and hotels you can get everything to drink. Wine is relatively expensive.

Waterfalls

Sai Rung / Pak Weep Waterfall (Rainbow Waterfall)

Sai Rung is the best accessible waterfall of Khao Lak. The road turns off Highway 4 just north of Bang Niang at kilometer 71 approximately 500 meters behind the entrance to the hotel "Le Meridien Beach Resort", or across the street at the height of kilometer 72. Now take the small concrete road and follow the sign "Rainbow Waterfall" (for 1 to 2 km) and then turn right. After another 1.6 km you reach the parking lot at the end of the road. After only a short (5 minute) walk you are there.

The 60 meter waterfall has a broad step at 20 meters from the bottom, which lets the water cascade down quite impressively. It is almost always possible to take a cool bath here because the waterfall has always water and there is still water in the lower pool even at the end of the high season (April). This makes the waterfall a popular Sunday destination for many Thai families.

DG 8.74143 98.27988
GMS   N 8° 44' 29.148" O 98° 16' 47.568"

Ton Chong Fa Waterfall / 5 stepped in the National park

You access the 5-step Ton Chong Fah waterfall, which is fed from the Bang Niang Canal, by the small road that branches off Highway 4 at kilometer 62.7. Follow the road to the sign for the

"Chong Fah Waterfall" and then turn right. After another 5 km you come across a barrier: the entrance to Lamru National Park, where the waterfall is located. After paying entry (adults 200 baht, Children 100 baht) you can proceed to the car park.

After a fairly strenuous walk (but at least through shady forest) of about 15-20 minutes you get to the first cascade of the 200 meter waterfall. If you want to go further up, keep right. There is a small path signposted near the waterhole. It is worthwhile in any case, because at the top fifth stage, the water drops down more than 20 m and with a little luck you can observe rare swallowtails or other pretty butterflies, insects and birds.

Ton Chong Fa Waterfall has water all year round, so you can have a cooling shower or bath in the knee- to waist-deep waterholes.

Bathing is still possible due to the prevailing water in the large water hole of the second cascade even at the end of the high season in April.

The waterfall is pretty – but this is the only place in Khao Lak where we have picked up leeches. . As they often sit in the bushes you not necessarily need to be in the water to pick one up. They are pretty gross, but not dangerous. Actually, they are a sign for a natural, unpolluted environment. To remove the leeches, either wait until they are full and drop off by themselves (after about 20 minutes) or scrape them off close to the skin.

DG 8.65626 98.28714
GMS   N 8° 39' 22.536" O 98° 17' 13.703"

By the way, with the entrance ticket you can visit Lam Ru National Park several times within the following 72 hours, for example to take the short coastal walk or to visit the Lam Ru waterfall.

Lampi Waterfall

(Pictured on the next side) To get to Lampi Waterfall, which is located about 30 minutes south of Khao Lak, follow the road that turns off Highway 4 at kilometer 33. The path from the parking lot to the waterfall is short, about 5 minutes by foot. It is a nice 3 - stage waterfall, best visited in the morning or late evening. The pool under the waterfall is deep enough to have a swim. The locals also come here for swimming and washing their clothes in the cascades. There are always people here as the waterfall is a popular stop after several tours.

DG 8.46443 98.28009
GMS   N 8° 27' 51.948" O 98° 16' 48.324"

Ton Prai Waterfall

Only a little further south is this 3-stage waterfall, which can be reached after a tiring (but only 650 m long) ascending walk through the jungle. The path is well posted, but leads over roots, a bamboo bridge, stones and in some places concrete. The waterfall is relatively quiet and not so crowded. Sometimes, a full parking lot may be misleading as the lot is also used by a nearby campsite. The road from Highway 4 goes off 30 km south of Khao Lak. Take the well signposted road at the Haadson Resort. Follow the road that gets more and more narrow and thickly wooded for 6 kilometers. At the visitor center you have to pay an entrance fee, as this is also part of the Lam Ru National Park.

DG 8.43654 98.30888
GMS   N 8° 26' 11.544" O 98° 18' 31.968"

Lam Ru Waterfall

The very pretty and easily accessible Lam Ru Waterfall is located 35 km from Khao Lak, near the village of Kapong. The waterfall belongs to the (eastern) part of the Lam Ru National Park.

You drive south on the Petchakasem Road (Highway 4, towards Phuket) and turn left at the major junction towards Thung Maphrao onto Highway 4240. Then follow the road to the next major intersection and turn left onto Highway 4090. Follow the road and turn right after about 15 km onto the small, freshly paved side road to "Lumru Waterfall" – the way is only signed in Thai. You could also drive up to Kapong and follow the English signs from there back south again to the Waterfall, but this way is faster.

After 4.5 km a sign for "Lamru Waterfall 800 m" points to the right into a narrow gravel and concrete road.

There is a barrier into Lam Ru National Park, where you may have to pay (100 baht for Children / 200 baht per adult), but whenever we visited in March or April the barrier was open and no one to be seen. You can park in the small parking lot a little further down. After a two-minute walk right past the small dam you reach the fall.

The 7-stage waterfall, which has its origins in the Kapong channel and is embedded in lush green surrounding with bamboo, rattan, palms and ferns, has water all year round. Over a narrow footpath on the right you can walk up to the highest level, where you can swim. The stage there is completely horizontal, like a wading pool.

DG 8.43654 98.30888
GMS   N 8° 26' 11.544" O 98° 18' 31.968"

Picture: Lam Ru Waterfall

Hin Lahd Waterfall

Hin Lahd waterfall is located 8 km north of Lam Ru waterfall. It is fed by three rivers.

Apart from the crystal clear waters and the rocky back wall that looks like it was built with bricks, the waterfall offers nothing spectacular. It is a meeting place for the children of the neighboring villages, who come here to cool down in hot weather.

DG 8.65697 98.46211
GMS   N 8° 39' 25.092" O 98° 27' 43.595"

Tam Nang Waterfall in the Sri Phang Nga National Park

And finally a real find: the waterfall in the Sri Phang Nga National Park, just 30 minutes north of Khao Lak. Take Highway 4 through Takua Pa. Where it divides you do not go to the right (to Khao Sok National Park), but proceed straight ahead in the direction of Ranong. About 40 km north of Takua Pa is another National Park: Sri Phang Nga. It seems the hordes of tourists have not yet discovered the park, even though there is the most fantastic waterfall.

The way to the National Park is well signed and goes off Highway 4 to the right. The road gets quite narrow when you proceed into the park, but do not let that put you off. There is an entrance fee (100 baht?). At the main entrance there is a sign that the waterfall is located about 1.5 km away ... but you can drive most of the way to it. Proceed until you reach a parking lot where you find a mini-stand with fish food you should buy as well (for about 20 baht).

Follow the well-signed path down to the river, where a lot of fish are waiting for you to feed them. But do not get rid of all the fish food because you can use some later. After a walk of about 10 minutes up and down through the green jungle you get to the large Sri Tamnang waterfall, which is 63 meters high (according to the park site) and perhaps the largest in the area, including Phuket. Amazingly, it is visited very sparsely, besides us there were only some locals. We had the waterfall to ourselves for over an hour, until at about 12 o'clock a few more Thai visitors showed up. You can swim in the rock pool below the waterfall with the same big fish as in the river below.

The waterfall is definitely worth a visit, even if you have to walk a bit more ...

Tam Nang Waterfall in Sri Phang Nga Ntl Park (pictured below)
DG 8.99635 98.46823
GMS   N 8° 59' 46.86"   O 98° 28' 5.628"

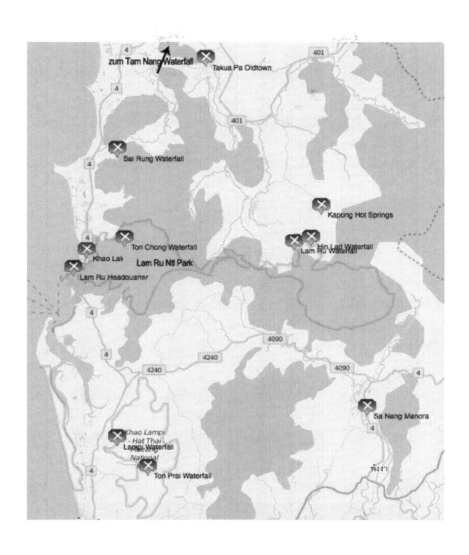

Overview Map of Waterfalls near Khao Lak.

Lam Ru National Park

Lam Ru National Park is 125 km^2 in size, ranging from the sea in the west to the hilly hinterland in the east. It is named after its two **highest elevations: Lak and Lam Ru**. On the way to Khao Lak you cross a small part of it when you drive over the hill. The park headquarters are located about 50 meters off Highway 4, towards the sea. The road there is signposted and goes off on the top of the hill.

DG 8.62685 98.23904
GMS   N 8° 37' 36.66"   O 98° 14' 20.544"

At the headquarters there is also the start of a short 3 km **Nature Trail** along the cape with scenic views of the coast, the sea and a beautiful beach. The walk takes you about 1 hour. Make sure to have enough water with you and bring sturdy shoes – even if the path is not challenging at the start. At the Visitor Centre there is an open-air restaurant overlooking the sea.

The park has several other trails, for example the **Namtok Ton Fa Nature Trail**, which is 5 km or 7 km long (approximately 2 respectively 5 hours). However, you will need a guide (a park ranger) if you want to do this trail.

Chong Fa Waterfall in Khao Lak is located in the western part of the park, **Lam Ru and Hin Lad waterfall** at **Kapong** in the eastern end of the park.

The **hot springs of Kapong** are located just outside the National Park.

There is an admission fee to the park, but the ticket can be used for 72 hours – also for other park entries.

Kapong and Hot Springs

Between Khao Lak and the interior lies a very hilly and wooded area, through which there are no roads yet. Those who want to go to Kapong (or Lam Ru waterfall) always have to make a detour to the north or to the south. But you can combine this detour into a pleasant half-day tour through the green countryside and see some of the attractions there.

From Khao Lak you drive south on Highway 4 (for about 15.5 km) to the big junction. Turn left onto the 4240 to Thung Maphrao. Follow the road to the next major junction, where you take the 4090 to the north.

(Those brave enough and with a good map, or satnav, can take the 4003, a narrow, paved village road and drive through uncommonly beautiful, rural areas until you also reach the 4090).

Coming from the 4240 take the newly made asphalt road to the right (entrance: DG 8.64169 98.40947 / GMS N 8° 38' 30.084" O 98° 24' 34.091") on the 4090 after about 15 km. The sign is unfortunately only written in Thai, but leads to **Lamru Waterfall** (see previous chapter). Otherwise, you can go straight to Kapong and follow the well-advertised signs back to the waterfall from there.

Next on the road is the small **village of Kapong**. In the village of Kapong, a large market takes place in a side street on the left on Sunday morning. Kapong itself is a very untouristy Thai village.

The **Wat Inthaphum** in Kapong has a Chedi Stupa and Naga (Snake) stairs and Chinese (fat) Buddha and is worth a stop.

DG 8.68917 98.40814
GMS   N 8° 41' 21.012" O 98° 24' 29.304"

You drive past the temple to the northern end of the town, where road 3002 turns north with the signs "Park Weep Waterfall 3 km" and "Hotsprings 8 km" the (good).

Follow the "**Hot Spring**" signs (sometimes written amusingly false) to the 5014, where you turn right. Stay on that road until it ends somewhat abruptly. The hot springs are not signposted there anymore, but they are right there, just turn right and drive down 500 m on the gravel road. Almost boiling water gushes into the riverbed, where it mixes with cold water, so that farther down below you can take a footbath. With a good car you can drive on the dirt road right to (and into) the river. There are also possibilities to park your car (not signposted) .

DG: 8.66979 98.47132
GMS N 8° 49' 11.244" O 98° 28' 16.752"

Takua Pa Old Town

To continue the tour above, go back to the 3002 and keep following it north until it meets the 401. There you turn left and follow it for about 4 km, then turn left to the 4090, drive over a bridge and then turn right into the 4032. Follow that road past the turn off (on the left) for 4005 directly into the old town of Takua Pa.

DG 8.82838, 98.36347
GSM N 8° 49' 42.168" O 98° 21' 48.492"

Takua Pa is the largest trading center in the region and more town than village. The **Old Town** is a bit hidden, but worth seeing. As most cities it is best seen on foot. Old Chinese-style arcade houses characterize the townscape. Every second or third year in September the nearby river floods the city for a few days and the waterlevel reaches up to one meter. The buildings suffer, but the houses still spread a certain morbid charm. With murals, Chinese home shrines and the work of the people living here, the place is a little gem. At the end of the road, there is a big **Chinese temple**.

A historic **street market** takes place every Sunday afternoon in Old Takua Pa in the high season. Some tourist tours will visit there then.

It is very worthwhile to stroll around and to try some of the unusual snacks and breathe in the atmosphere.

The quickest way back to Khao Lak is by the new **Pakweep Street**, the 4005. Although it is new, it has some treacherous potholes. Nevertheless, it is a scenic drive that takes you 23.2 kilometers through green forests and plantations to the west and to Highway 4 (at km 71.8). From there it is only 11.8 km back to Khao Lak.

Orchid Garden und Butterfly Farm Khao Lak

Somewhat hidden and slightly off Highway 4 is a small sign that leads you over a short (unpaved) road to the Orchid Garden and Butterfly Farm. .Winding paths and fluttering butterflies are guiding you through a tropical garden to the orchid collection.

These pretty flowers are one of the largest groups of plants and are found in many places over the world. Thailand is well-known for them and is home to over 1100 species. This makes for a pretty little detour or something to squeeze it in between other trips. In the souvenir shop you can buy many orchid- and butterfly-related souvenirs. Perfume, magnets, carved soap, and of course orchids themselves – which one may take back home with the provided certificate.

Open daily from 9 am to 5 pm from November to the end of April. Admission is 100 baht for the orchid farm and 150 baht for the butterflies.

Directions: Coming from Phuket you take Highway 4 to the north past the Bang Niang Beach road and past La Flora and the Market on the left. Further up, after a slight right turn you see a petrol station on the left. The entrance is on the right side of the road, opposite the petrol station – between km 64 and 65. you can drive all the way up to the farm.

DG 8.69411 98.25682
GMS   N 8° 41' 38.796" O 98° 15' 24.552"

Khao Lak Minigolf

This is something to do with the family if you want to get a change from the beach. The course is surrounded by green plants and tropical landscapes. The trees give shade and in between the holes there bubbles a small stream. There is an "ancient temple" and the minigolf course is well maintained (though obviously a bit older).

Location: at the road to the Chong Fah Waterfall, Bang Niang Beach. (Signed)

Khao Lak Turtle Sanctuary

The **Phang Nga Coastal Fisheries Research and Development Center** (also known as Turtle Heaven) was founded 1985. At first it was only a research station and the aim was to breed mussels and shrimp. In 2002 it was reconstructed into the present center.

The aim of the center is to accommodate a wide range of marine life to breed and protect them. For this purpose they research out in the sea in the area and set for example rules for fishing. They also look for ways to get the animals to breed (for commercial purposes).

Here you can have a look at various species of turtles (and fish, crabs, giant clams, starfish and more) in large saltwater tanks made of concrete. It appears a little ... rough, but does the job and the animals that can be found here are really special.

In the center are four species of turtles which are endangered today: Green turtle Riddley turtle Hawksbill turtle and Leatherback turtle. These are species that can be found in the Andaman Sea, especially around the Similan and Surin Islands. They hatched and spend the first few months here until they are released when about 8 months old. By making a donation you can release a turtle on the beach yourself – if you are there at the right time, early March. There are also tanks for the sick and injured animals that they look after and keep there.

Location: The Center is found on the road along the Thai Muang beach, about 30 km south of Khao Lak. The take off for this road is in the village of Thai Muang on Highway 4 – you drive through the large metal gate (which is next to the Chinese gate) rather than follow the curve of the main road.

DG 8.42029 98.24212
GMS   N 8° 25' 13.044" O 98° 14' 31.631"

Temples and Religion

There is no official state religion in Thailand and they have freedom of religion, but 95% of the population belongs to the Theravada Buddhism – the king even by law. Buddhism in Thailand has a strong undercurrent of Hinduism and a Thai-Chinese part practice diverse Chinese folk religions including Taoism. In the south of Thailand, a part of the population (mostly Malays) are Muslims and make up about 5% of the total population. Only about 1% are Christians.

Buddhist monks can bee seen walking through the streets especially in the morning. They usually have a bowl with them, in which they receive food donations. Women cannot be monks (or nuns) in Theravada Buddhism, but many men have spent some time as a novice in a monastery as boys – formerly the only way to reach a (higher) education. Today, there is an education system run by the state, but the schools often still cooperate with the temples and monks.

The temples are open to visit for everyone (also tourists), but you should behave respectfully. Wear decent clothes: miniskirts or shorts and tops with spaghetti straps are not okay, neither is going shirtless for men.

Take off your shoes before entering the temple. In the temples there are often shoe racks, but you can also simply place your shoes on the floor in front of the entrance.

Do not step on the doorstep as the house ghost lives there and stepping on its head brings misfortune.

Do not touch or climb the Buddha figures. In addition, as is already advertised at the airport, neither buy Buddha statues and images.

Take pictures respectfully – without flash and ask people in advance whether they agree.

However, the Thais are very easy going and forgiving regarding the behavior of the tourists ... and the atmosphere in the temples is often anything but subdued.

Temples in Khao Lak

Khao Lak has two large beautiful Thai temples, conveniently located on the Highway 4.

Wat Khomniyaket is located directly next to the entrance of the JW Marriott. It exibits fantastically decorated classic buildings and animal figures around it, which hint at the animistic part of religion, which is tolerated here.

DG 0.70597 98.25747
GMS   N 0° 42' 21.492" O 98° 15' 26.891"

Wat Pattikaram is located south of the hill Lak at Lampi Waterfall.

DG 8.44248 98.25738
GMS   N 8° 26' 32.928" O 98° 15' 26.567"

There are some very nice temples to visit a little further south: **in Phang Nga**. To get there just follow Highway 4 to the south and instead of turning right to Phuket you turn left onto Phang Nga.

Wat Suwan Kuha

It is sometimes also called Wat Suwannakuha or Wat Tham, also known as **"the Temple with the Great Buddha in the cave"**.

Amazingly, the turn-off of Highway 4 (to the left) is not signed, or at least not in English. But it does have a sign for the Raman Waterfall National Forest – just follow this one. After about half a kilometer you get to the large parking lot of the temple on the right.

DG 8.42884 98.47056
GMS   N 8° 25' 43.824" O 98° 28' 14.016"

The entrance to the cave with the Buddha is on the right side of the parking lot through a beautiful (blue) painted gate.

Quite a lot of tours and tourists visit this temple, which is why there is a whole infrastructure of small shops in the parking lot. Besides drinks, ice-cream, t-shirts and other souvenirs you can also buy peanuts for the many monkeys here. But take care, the monkeys are quite obtrusive – tour guides use slingshots to keep them at bay, individual tourists must be attentive so that the monkeys do not steal anything.

In the cave itself (you pay entrance), you can see the 15-meter long reclining Buddha statue and some smaller golden statues. There is also the opportunity to be told your future by a machine – which unfortunately is only in Thai ...

A staircase leads upstairs (and outside) at the back of the cave. Follow the staircase to get to a plateau where another staircase on the left leads down to a pretty limestone cave

Wat Thamtapan

This temple is a little ... different. It is located at the end of Soi Thamtapan, a small side street in Phang Nga. At first you may

think you have surprisingly landed in a somewhat abstract Disneyland. But there are not only animal figures, but also disturbing statues of how the Thai imagine hell.

You will descend to hell by a **dragon mouth** (and a long passage going downhill behind it) – or if you take the path on the left along the rock wall – to a monk in a semi-cave, which will bless even a farang (non-Thai) for a corresponding return gift.

Buddhist Hell is called Narok in Thai. If you see its images here, you understand that it is a good idea to be "good" in life.

If you go past the dragon and to the back of the temple area, you find a row of commemorative statues of monks on the left and a large stone relief on the rock wall. On the right, tucked behind the huts, there is a wobbly and steep staircase going up to a viewing platform and a shrine on the top of the hill.

DG 8.45393, 98.52807
N 8° 27' 14.148" O 98° 31' 41.051"

Wat Bang Riang - Pagoda Temple:

This temple is also called **Wat Rat Upatam**. It is located on the top of a hill and includes a combination of three different temple styles: Thai, Chinese and Chedi pagoda. A tooth of Buddha is kept in a shrine. The temple is located quite far from the coast, 40km north of Phang Nga. A large seated golden Buddha statue high on the hill is looking over the country. There are a lot of stairs, but the view over the green hills is worthwhile. The temple is visited mainly by Thai tourists and some tours, but still worth seeing.

DG 8.59346, 98.66891
N 8° 35' 36.456" O 98° 40' 8.075"

3 Temple Tour

Many tour operators offer 3-Temple tours, sometimes with different temples. They include almost always Wat Suwan Kuha in the cave and frequently Bang Riang on the hill.

This is a full day tour, including transfers, temple entrance fees and lunch / beverages and some information on religion in Thailand.

Pick up from the hotel is in the morning and you drive to the temples (by van), where you can learn something about the religion and history. In between the temples, there is a nice lunch in a Thai restaurant. In the evening you will be brought back.

Because the temples are somewhat removed (especially Wat Bang Riang) this tour includes a lot of driving, which is why it is not best suited for children. But you can also do a tour by yourself and put it together differently.

Ghost houses

Many houses in Thailand have these little houses or shrines in front of them – mostly on stilts or a pedestal. The size varies from shoebox size to the size of a small single-family home. These are ghost houses, the shrines for the nature spirits in Thailand. They are actually the remnants of the old animistic faith, which is tolerated by Buddhism.

Once a house is built at a site, these are erected to appease the ghosts living there. But they are also found next to accident-prone roads. The spirits receive sacrifices in the form of food and drink and the style of the houses is often more attractive than the main building – so that the spirits do no move there.

Phang Nga

The **city Phang Nga** itself is not very remarkable. Economically, it currently seems to be on the rise – there is a lot of building going on. It does not have an Old Town, but it has plenty of opportunities for accommodation and also some restaurants. The city is surrounded by green hills and close to the mangrove coast and serves primarily as a starting point for tours to the Phang Nga Bay and its attractions.
If you do not want to book a tour, you can rent a boat and guide at **Surakul Pier.**

Pier: DG: 8.39005, 98.46033DG   8.39005 98.46033
GMS   N 8° 23' 24.18"   O 98° 27' 37.187"

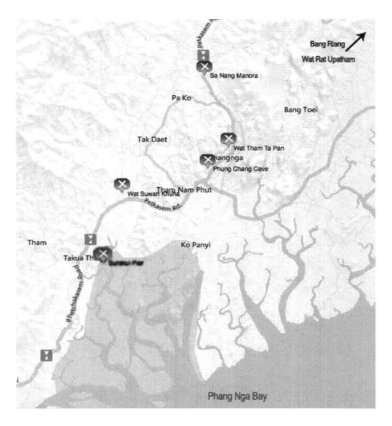

Phung Chan Cave

Not a Temple, but nearby is Phung Chan Cave or **Elephant Belly Cave.** The rock in which it is looks like a (petrified) Elephant ... so the cave is in the belly. Logical, right?

For 500 baht you can take a 30-40 minute tour on which some of the interesting rock formations are shown. A large part of the tour takes place on the water: you move around by kayak, bamboo raft or wading, so it is advisable to wear shorts and water resistant shoes.

Location: This is also just a little off the Highway 4 – if you continue into Phang Nga itself.

DG 8.44217 98.51684
GMS   N 8° 26' 31.812" O 98° 31' 0.624"

Sa Nang Manora Waterfall Forest Park

About 5 kilometers north of Phang Nga is this **Park**, which has several waterfalls and caves. Follow the signs and the road off Highway 4 to the right (if you come from the south).

A 2 km **nature trail**, a **Bat Cave** and a **Shell Cave** are posted in the park.

You reach a couple of pools and waterfalls after a short walk through the trees. On a hot day this is a nice detour to take a picnic and cool down. The waterfalls are not spectacular, but with its green setting and the tranquility, this is a small paradise.

DG 8.49414 98.51524
GMS   N 8° 29' 38.904" O 98° 30' 54.864"

Phang Nga Bay Tour

This wonderful, large bay (401 km^2 is the part of the National Park alone) with mangrove forests on the shores and steep karst formations (limestone hills) protruding from the water is only an hour by car from Khao Lak.

The best-known part is Koh Tapu – commonly known as James Bond Island – but there are other beautiful rock formations, caves and rock paintings.

Phang Nga Bay is a UNESCO World Heritage Site. Originally it was shaped from the coral deposits of an ancient sea, which was raised by folding and then largely removed again by erosion. It has thus the same origin as Halong Bay in Vietnam with the iconic landscape – and it shows. There are 42 islands in the bay and the unique views attracts many tourists every year. I would advise here to book a tour or a guide to visit.

An example of a day tour:

Morning pick-up at hotel is around 8 am (the exact time will be announced when booking) and then you drive south – about 1 hour, to a small pier in the mangroves in Phang Nga Bay.

Depending on the tides you ride in a long-tail boat through the mangroves ... not all waterways are open at low tide. The sea here is only a few meters deep – a reason why there are hardly any high waves in the bay. Nevertheless, it is good to protect your camera and other electrical appliances from the water.

Ko Tapu – James Bond Island

The first stop is usually Ko Tapu or (as it is called) **James Bond Island.** The 20 m high rock that stands lonely in the sea was shown prominently in the 1974 James Bond film "The Man with the Golden Gun"... But those who hope to find the hiding place or the great Villa of the villain Scaramanga here are disappointed. It even cannot be found in the crevice with the commemorative plaque. A narrow path leads up on the right side and halfway around the island to the remains of a pier (which has been washed away) and a small sandy beach.

In the middle of the island a lot of small souvenir shops have been erected, where you can also get ice-cream or something to drink. One should take care not to buy shells and coral on offer here – it is forbidden to take them out of Thailand.

You are never alone here ... except maybe if you organize a private tour in the evening – after 5 pm, when island is left by everybody.

Kayaking in the Phang Nga Bay

You continue your day tour by long-tail boat to a canoe station, which consists of a bigger ship fixed near some cliffs with caves. There you get a canoe and can paddle with a guide for about 30 to 45 minutes through the mangroves and caves.

Embark the long-tail boat again and to see some paintings on the rock walls: fish, dolphins and geometric structures. Unfortunately, the age of the drawings is unknown.

Koh Panyi – Sea gypsy village

In the fishing village of Koh Panyi you have a small guided walking tour. The 300 year-old village is almost completely built on stilts; only a small part (where the mosque stands) is on the land. On the sea side of the fishing village there is a row of tourist-restaurants and a variety of shops inside. They even have a soccer field on the water!

In spite of the precarious location not one of the inhabitants perished in the 2004 Tsunami. Some elders who knew what it means when the sea retracts, warned everybody and the villagers fled to higher ground.

Back on the mainland you visit the cave temple with monkeys: **Wat Suwanakhua**.

Included in the tour: transfers, national park fees, life jackets (especially for children), lunch and (non-alcoholic) drinks, guide.

Things to bring: sunscreen, hat (at least for the canoe trip, but also otherwise), camera in a waterproof bag, towel, and bathing gear.

Phang Nga Bay on a Chinese Junk

A trip for romantic moments is a the **Sunset Dinner Cruise**, which is a dinner **aboard a Chinese junk** in the picturesque Phang Nga Bay with the sun going down.

Pick up from the hotel is in the late afternoon. You are driven to the Marina in (northern) Phuket. Dinner is served on June Bahtra, a traditional Chinese junk. In the evening, the bay is practically deserted (by tourists and locals) and provides beautiful views at sunset.

Then you will disembark at the Marina again and be brought back to your hotel.

Tsunami 2004 Museum, Boat and Memorial

Khao Lak was one of the regions hit hardest by the tsunami which occurred after the earthquake in the Indian Ocean in December of 2004. Much of the landscape on the coast was destroyed. The local economy was also severely affected. At that time many resorts were under construction and were destroyed by the tsunami. That and the loss of over 4000 human lives–(compare to Phuket: 300 victims) was a huge throwback to the rising tourism economy.

However, Khao Lak has meanwhile recovered – the resorts as well as the local infrastructure have been rebuilt and the population independent from tourism is again on a level as before the tsunami.

Navy Boat 813

A lasting memory of the tsunami provides the Navy Boat 813, which was pushed onto the land by the wave and is still there – now as a monument.

The boat was anchored off the coast, and had the task to protect a member of the royal family, the grandson of the king, who was jet skiing in front of Khao Lak. The power of the tsunami has torn the almost 25-meter long boat loose and carried it over one kilometer inland. The grandson was killed, his mother, Princess Ubolratana was ashore and had to take refuge with others in the upper floors of the La Flora resort, where they survived.

The large Navy boat is still in the same place where it was stranded – almost 2 km inland from the sea. It was left there as a memorial – and over the years the area has been developed. Earlier the boat lay on its side, almost lonely in a wide, green field; today it has been stabilized and the field paved. Plaques commemorate the incident.

Location: inland, somewhat off Highway 4, opposite the Bang Niang market. Meanwhile, it is no longer as clearly visible from the street because there are new houses being built.

DG 8.66649 98.25469
GMS   N 8° 39' 59.364" O 98° 15' 16.883"

Tsunami Museum

The International Tsunami Museum is near the memorial, on the Highway 4 (just north). On 2 levels there are small, fairly barren rooms with photos and videos running continuously with information about tsunamis in general and the 2004 tsunami and the impact on Khao Lak and the surrounding area in particular.

Some of these films I have seen on YouTube before. They are accounts and recordings of eyewitness, which impressively show what power this wave had ... and that it is not, as one often imagines, a meter-high tidal wave, but an unstoppable force. The reason it is so dangerous is because it takes lot of debris with it, crushing everything and destroying more than water alone would.

Tsunami Memorial in Baan Nam Khen

A site particularly affected was the fishing village of Baan Nam Khen, north of the beaches of Khao Lak. It is now the site of Baan Nam Khem Tsunami Memorial Park, just west of the village (and piers to Ko Kho Khao) on the beach. The park is well maintained and has a small museum with many photos. The memorial consists of two longer walls that face each other. One is concrete and shaped like a big wave; the opposite wall is covered with tiles, some with photos, others with fresh flowers. A wall full of names of people who ceased to exist, but who have not been forgotten include some European names.

Location: At the headland near the pier to the island of Ko Kho Khao.

DG 8.85919 98.26523/
GMS N 8° 51' 33.084"O 98° 15' 54.828"

Tsunami Warning system

Because of the tsunami a warning system was set up. It faced a test in April 2012 and successfully passed it: after an earthquake off Sumatra it issued a warning about 2 hours before the wave – enough time for everyone to reach higher ground.

Signs indicating the evacuation routes can be seen in many places on the coast today ... even if some of them are pretty faded by now.

Ko Kho Khao

North of Khao Lak, almost at the level of Takua Pa, is an island that is only a 10-minute boat ride from the mainland and has gained tourist upswing. On Ko Kho Khao you find the tourists (and families) who are looking for a beach destination in Thailand that is not too hard to reach, but is still quiet. Ko Kho Khao is that for sure – the long golden beaches are its main attraction. They look like those further down south in Khao Lak. The water is not as clear or has the animal life that can be found at the Similan or Surin Islands, but you can swim there, walk along the beach and enjoy a romantic sunset.

The island is about 16 km long and consists mainly of sandy beaches in the west, flat, grassy hills in the middle and mangroves and canals in the east. There are now a number of hotels and infrastructure with taxis and restaurants. The busiest place is still at the pier.

In the far north on the island there is a larger (grass) field, which was used by the Japanese as an airfield during World War II. Today they are discussing the construction an airport there again. Ko Kho Khao also has ruins of an ancient seafaring settlement, which can be visited: Mueng Thong. Several artifacts have been found there: clay pots, glass, stone beads and Buddha images. It was clearly a center for international trade between China and the Middle East.

Ko Kho Khao is more a place to be than to visit, but those who want to, can do so by going to the pier near the village of Bang Muang and take the ferry there (or one of the smaller water taxis) to the island for little money. Anyone traveling by motorbike or bicycle can also transfer it.

DG 8.86554 98.27409 / GMS N 8° 51' 55.944" O 98° 16' 26.724"

Dive- und Snorkel-Tours

Long before it was a known tourist destination, Khao Lak was an insider tip for divers and snorkelers. The now well known beautiful dive sites are situated off the coast: the nine **Similan Islands, Koh Bon** (20 km north of Similan), **Koh Tachai** (45 km north), **Richelieu Rock** (85 km north), the **Surin Islands** and **wrecks** like the Boonsung, Premchai and Sea Chart.

Trips and diving courses can be booked at many places in Khao Lak. The range goes from half-day excursions to multi-day trips where you stay on the dive boat.

Diving is a wonderful sport and it can be very rewarding to pick it up. To be able to experience the underwater world so close (and for so long) is wonderful – so it is worth learning it where you have access to such great dive sites.

When choosing a diving center or diving course, make sure that they are PADI or SSI qualified. To really learn it, you have to invest some days and learn the theory correctly as well as going out to dive. Anyone who is uncertain can try a (one-day) introductory course – after which you go diving at the Similan Islands down to 12 meters deep.

The prices are not cheap, however you have to bear in mind that the courses include material (snorkel, fins, mask, suit, bottle, vest), the study materials and guided excursions to the dive sites: 1 day is about 6000 baht. Open Water courses including a local half-day tour and a 1-day tour to the Similan cost about 15,000 baht

Children from the age of 8 can do an introductory course in the pool (to 2 m depth), the Bubble Maker. They are accompanied and instructed by parents and an experienced instructor. Price: about 1500 baht. Minimum age for Junior Diving courses is 10-12 years.

Similan Islands

The Similan Island Marine National Park is located about 70 km off the coast from Khao Lak. It includes 140 km^2 and 9 islands, but only 2 of them are accessible for tourists: Islands No. 4 and 8. On these islands there is some infrastructure like toilets and a restaurant and they are the destination of many day-trip tourists. These trips can be booked at various locations: at the hotel, on the Internet, on site in one of the local tour agencies in Khao Lak, in diving centers and (sometimes) in a restaurant in Khao Lak itself.

DG 8.65786 97.64667
GMS   N 8° 39' 28.296" O 97° 38' 48.012"

The course of a day trip to snorkel / for sightseeing is as follows:

You are picked up at the hotel at the lobby (time: early in the morning, depending on how many other hotels are to be approached by one van, between 7 am to 9 am).

You will be taken to the pier – mostly to Thap Lamu (in the south), occasionally to Bang Muang (in the north), depending on tour organizer and the tide. At the port you will be equipped with snorkel, mask and flippers (everything in your size and also for children). Before the boat ride there is a short introduction about the islands you are about to visit and the diving / snorkeling sites. You have the opportunity to take a pill against seasickness offered for free (active ingredient: dimenhydrinate 50mg). I highly recommend it if you are prone to seasickness: the speedboat ride can be very bumpy if the wind picks up.

On the boat you have to wear a lifejacket. There are better seats and worse ... in the front part of the boat you may have a nice view, but are in the blazing sun. You cannot talk much because of the engine noise, but there are free drinks and occasionally you can already see flying fish.

After an hour you arrive at the island with beautiful round rock formations and turquoise waters with lots of colorful fish and coral.

You now snorkel at a site close to the island. If you are lucky you see turtles (some of the tours feed them bananas so they return here) and certainly you can see corals and lots of colorful fish. A disposable underwater camera or waterproof case is worth bringing here.

The water is warm, usually around 30 degrees Celsius and the visibility mostly good – unless there is a lot of wind.

After snorkeling (each stop is about 30 - 45 minutes and you have 2 or 3 of them on a trip) you head for the "main island" with its white beach. Every excursion boat moors at that place, so it is quite busy ... and you have to watch out while in the water.

The island has a viewpoint: **Sail Rock**, which is relatively easily accessible. Just a short climb that you can do barefoot – but because this is literally a "hot thing" on the sun-baked rocks, it is better to take trekking sandals with you (waterproof if possible).

Lunch is on the island along with the other tourists. There is a (quite decent) buffet and after that you have the possibility to take a rest before you have to find your speedboat to head for another snorkeling stop. During the transfers you always get fruit and drinks on board. Everything is taken care of.

Back at the pier you return your snorkel gear (and pay for lost material), are allocated to a van and return to the hotel.

Equipment needed: sun screen (high-factored and water-resistant), bath towels, swimming gear (already wear it, so you do not have to change), T-shirt and pants at will, (water-resistant) trekking sandals, camera (possibly with waterproof shell).

The National Park is closed from May 1 to October 31.

Koh Tachai

The island is located north of the Similan Islands and has been part of the same National Park since 2012. (DG 9.06903, 97.81096). In contrast to the Similan Islands you will find fewer tourists here ... though the island and the water around are at least as beautiful. There is a dazzling beach with white sand:

You can also book day trips to here; they start at about the same time as the ones to the Similan Islands. The transfer time depends on which port is used: Between 1 hour from the northern port and 90 minutes from the south.

Snorkeling is possible right off the beach, but you have to swim out further to see anything because the water is very shallow here and the boats are kicking up the sand, which affects visibility.

But if you go just a few steps up the beach and away from the other visitors there is the place to really get that "tropical desert island feeling".

Lunch is offered on the island – a rich Thai buffet as well. After your visit to the island you once more transfer to a snorkel spot and are back at the pier at about 5 pm.

Surin Islands

Even further north are the Surin Islands, which belong to the best diving sites in Thailand (with the Similan Islands) with an incredible underwater world and which are also within easy reach from Khao Lak. You cannot stay on the islands, but day trips or liveaboard (that is where you stay on the dive boat) are worth it, despite the lack of comfort.

DG 9.43438 97.86811
GMS   N 9° 26' 3.768"   O 97° 52' 5.196"

Day trip: Pick up from the hotel is around 7 am. You are driven to the pier and taken by Speed Boat to the Surin Islands. Snorkeling at Maeyai Bay at Chong Kard. Lunch is on the island of Chong Kard. Visit the Moken village (sea gypsies on an isolated island). Snorkeling on Ao Tao and Pak Kard. Relax on the beach, then you are driven back to the pier and transferred to the hotel. Back about 6 pm.

For all these trips to the islands west of the coast of Khao Lak and the diving / snorkeling sites it is worthwhile to have a look at the weather before booking Wind (or a storm) does not only make the crossing rougher, but also affects the visibility in the water. Also, you have to expect changes in the trip.

Takua Pa Mangroves – „little Amazon"

A half-day excursion you can book –sometimes it is integrated into longer tours. Pick up from the hotel in the morning is at about 9 am. The drive to Takua Pa takes approximately 30 minutes. From the pier you go on a guided kayak tour through the channels in the mangroves, passing Banyan trees and wetlands. On the tour you can observe diverse birds and reptiles such as snakes (resting on the trees), sometimes big lizards and frogs. You may also visit Takua Pa Old Town and a waterfall. Lunch is at a Thai restaurant and you get back to the hotel at 2 pm.

Bamboo Rafting

This is something to do as a romantic getaway or as a family with smaller children. The river on which you float down is not very fast and has little current. Sitting (with your bottom in the water) on the rustic bamboo rafts you glide along steered by the guide, watching the green forest and various plants, birds and butterflies.

Half-day trip: Pick up from the hotel is around 9 am in the morning. Transfer to Kiangkoo River. (This must be somewhere south, but not to be found on maps – perhaps they mean the Klang?). Bamboo rafting on the gentle river with wonderful views of the green rainforest. Then you visit the Sea Turtle Conservatory in Thai Muang. Swim at a waterfall to refresh and be back at the hotel at about 12 pm.

Attractions with Elephants

Asian elephants are endangered. Of the approximately 200,000 wild elephants in Siam in around 1900 there are only about 2000 left (by optimistic estimate). The animals, which were used for centuries as working animal for moving loads and in wars (the power of the ruler was measured by the number of elephants) are now replaced by machines. The Forest Protection Act in Thailand from 1989 left thousands of elephants and mahouts unemployed. The owners then tried to make money from the tourists with the elephants. An elephant consumes about 200 kilos of food a day and he must be moved, fed and entertained.

Many mahouts do that well and take good care of their animals. But of course, there are exceptions as well.

Nevertheless, attractions with elephants are seen controversial. You should remember that in spite of all the years of working for the humans, they are still wild animals, even if most are now raised in captivity and not kept in a near-natural environment. They cannot range free at night, they are trained with various, sometimes quite cruel methods. Therefore, unsuitable animals can occasionally be found at tourist attractions. Male elephants in the rutting season react aggressively. Accidents during elephant rides are therefore not that uncommon then.

If you (still) want to go elephant riding, you should have a look at how the elephants are treated. In case of bad treatment I would do without a ride. Here are some signs of mistreatment to look for:

- Does the elephant have scars or wounds at the joints, on the head or buttocks? These can be from the mahouts' equipment, which they control their elephants with. However, it is also possible that the elephants have been scratching on trees.

- Is there any powder (white or purple) at these locations? – powder is often used for wound care.

- Does the elephant constantly shake his head or does he have other behavioral problems?

- How is the condition of the farm? Do the elephants have enough space? When and where do the elephant rides take place? For example, it is also a torment for the elephants if they have to walk in the blazing sun without shade at lunchtime.

– Having said all that, we have gone elephant riding several times, which is always an experience. We have seen several providers, and only once in all the years we have not felt "comfortable": that was at the Khao Sok Park, with one of the largest suppliers there. There we had a fairly large (male?) Elephant and a mahout with a long rod with a sharp hook, who was getting visibly nervous when Junior came too close to the elephant during the subsequent feeding. A few weeks later in a tourist couple got injured the same park because two elephants started fighting with each other.

I therefore do not advise against elephant rides, but you should be respectful of the large animals and listen to your inner voice. If you do not want to get on the elephant as the third person, you can also walk alongside. An elephant should not carry more than 150 kg on its back. At lunchtime and in the blazing sun, I would not mount an elephant.

Besides riding, there are **other activities you can do with elephants:**

Having a bath with the elephant: there are different providers in Khao Lak – I recommend a good look before you go, otherwise you end up in a rather murky pond with the elephant instead of in clean flowing water.

It is also possible to **wash and clean an elephant**. We have discovered this a few years ago and since then have been preferring this to riding – it is offered in Khao Sok Park, bookable at Elephant Hills.

Khao Sok National Park

The very green National Park with a lake in a fantastic landscape is a popular tourist destination just north of Khao Lak (takes about 1 hour to get there) and Phuket (about 2 hours) and is also visited from Krabi and Ko Samui. The main focus is on eco-tourism and many activities are offered: elephant riding (and washing), jungle-trekking on foot, canoeing, bamboo raft riding, tubing, boat safaris ...

The 739 km^2 large national park is covered by the oldest rainforest in the world, contains steep limestone hills (between 400 to 960 m), deep valleys, breathtaking lakes, dark caves, wild animals and rare plants such as the Rafflesia – a very large carnivorous flower.

You can see the following wild animals there: hornbills, elephants, Asian oxen, monkeys, gibbons, snakes ...

The climate is often more humid and rainier than further South, even than in Khao Lak...

The park entrance fee is 300 baht (per day) for non-Thais. There are some paved roads, where you can also go hiking in the park, but for most of the tours you need a guide (park ranger).

Visitor Centre / Park Headquarters:
DG 8.91542 98.52809
GMS   N 8° 54' 55.512" O 98° 31' 41.124"

Accommodation in and at the national park is plentiful and of varying quality. You can book in the visitor center. Tours can also be booked directly with the landlord.

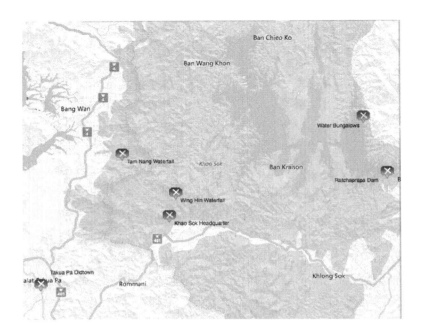

Hiking and Things to See in the National Park:

Nine trails begin at the visitor center. One of them leads to **Wing Hin Waterfall**, is 2.8 kilometers long (one way) and can be done without a guide. The path through the green park there is beautiful, if somewhat challenging and Wing Hin Waterfall ... not huge, but it is nice to bathe your feet beside the great stone boulders in the water and cool down before returning.

Other attractions in the park are only accessible with a guide:

Tang Nam: two high cliffs standing close to each other at the end of the Sok Channel. 6 km away from the headquarters, the way to Bang Wing Hin Waterfall continues to there.

Sip Et Chan Waterfall: stair-like waterfall over 11 steps with a large pool where you can swim. 4 km from the headquarters.

Ton Kloi Waterfall: about 7 km from the headquarters, on the Sok River.

Tharn Sawan Waterfall: Waterfall of a side creek of the Sok River. The path here is quite strenuous and the last kilometers go through the riverbed, where you have to wade.

Diamond Cave (Pra Kay Petch Cave): Cave with stalactites, huge spiders, bats and dark ... definitely take a flashlight.

Si Ru Cave: Cave with four entrances, 4 km away from the headquarters. Communist rebels formerly used it as a hideout.

Nam Ta-lu Cave: cave near the dam. Can be reached on a 2 km long path after a boat ride on the lake. 30 m wide entrance and a river that runs through the cave. Quite adventurous.

Khang Cow Cave: stalactite cave with thousands of bats.

Rafflesia Kerrii Meijer: giant flower, approximately 1 m in diameter. It is a parasitic plant that is very rare. It takes 9 months until it flowers and the flower keeps only about 7 days – so you have to be pretty lucky to see them.

May Yai Waterfall: The only waterfall of the National Park which can be reached by car. It is 5.5 km away from headquarters, alongside the Suratthani-Takuapa road (at km 113). Only single-stage, and about 30 m high. Best visited during the rain season, otherwise there may be little water.

Bang Hua Council Waterfall and **Lum Khlong Sok**: Rapids which interrupt the river like some steps. A popular place for river rafting.

Hikers should wear shoes that are sturdy and firmly closed. Sandals invite leeches that occur in the park on the ground and in the trees. Use of insect repellents is also recommended to somewhat fend off the leeches.

Guided evening / night trips offered here can be very beautiful as you can see nocturnal animals. Do not do this on your own – not only because you risk getting lost, but there are snakes here.

Kayaking (or Bamboo-Rafting) on the Sok River

The river Sok is the main river in the Khao Sok National Park. The link road 401 between Takua Pa and Surat Thani is located in its valley and crosses it several times. The river is surrounded by beautiful scenery with high limestone cliffs and greenery. Various activities such as kayaking or bamboo rafting are carried out on and in the river and its tributaries. The river is quite tame in the dry season (high season) and at the end of the dry season in April it may has very little water.

On the **quiet ride** along the river you can enjoy the landscape, see birds and monkeys, various amphibians and reptiles – but no crocodiles, even if the guides sometimes joke about that.

Some trips will stop for a tea or coffee (prepared on a fire next to the river) or for a swim. Occasionally there are ropes hanging from the trees, from where you can let yourself drop into the deeper parts of the river or feel like Tarzan. Fun for the whole family!

Cheow Lan Lake

Cheow Lan Lake, which is 165 km^2 large and about 200 m deep has a colorful history.

The park has steep limestone cliffs towering up to 900 m out of the water – a similar sight to the Phang Nga Bay, only with fresh water and almost more impressive, if that is possible.

The dam that created the lake was built 1982 to generate electricity for the (quickly) developing region.

Thailand's King named it **the Rajiaprabha dam** – the name means "the light of the kingdom" – in an opening ceremony on his 60th birthday. Except for generating electricity it also serves as flood control and is used for irrigation and fish farming. It took about one year for the lake to fill and nearly 400 families from a village had to be resettled. There were projects to resettle the animals by boat and helicopter – but many died because their habitat was so suddenly limited. Nevertheless, many partly endangered species can be found (again) in the national park and the lake today.

Dam: DG   8.97247 98.8057
GMS   N 8° 58' 20.892" O 98° 48' 20.52"

On the lake there are floating bungalows where you can stay overnight – the operators have to be relatives of the original landowners to get a license for it. The bungalows are of varying quality – from simple wooden huts to barrel-like floating modern rooms (with toilets on land) and luxury tents on rafts (with toilets inside the tents) … everything can be found here.

Examples of tours exploring Khao Sok Park:

Day trip Khao Sok

Pick up from hotel is around 8 am. Drive to the Khao Sok National Park with a stop at the local market (in Takua Pa). Elephant riding by a river. Feeding and photographing of the elephants. Stop at the Khao Sok viewpoint. Thai lunch. Afternoon kayaking on the Sok River. Swimming in the Sok River. Visit to a local temple with monkeys. Stop at a waterfall. Back at the hotel at approximately 5 pm.

2 - day trip Khao Sok / Park

Pick up from hotel around 8 am. Drive to the Khao Sok National Park with a stop at the local market (in Takua Pa). Elephant riding by a creek. Thai lunch. Afternoon kayaking on the Sok River. Swimming in the Sok River. Check in at your Bungalow at the park.

Day 2: Trekking in the Khao Sok National Park. Here you have the possibility to see gibbons, langurs, birds and various reptiles. Bathing under the waterfall. Back to the resort and lunch. Ride back after an afternoon rest.

It should be noted here that on these day tours you usually are on the edge of the national park and not in it – except if you visit the lake or go trekking to the interior with a guide. This means that the tour guides do not have to pay park fees, but the landscape is still worth seeing. You also do not notice that the main road passes practically right next to the Sok River.

2 - day trip Khao Sok / Lake

Drive to the Khao Sok National Park. Stop at the Viewpoint. Visit the headquarters. Drive to Cheow Lan Lake (Ratchaprapa Dam). Ride by longtail boat through the fantastic scenery. Arrive at raft house (floating hotel). Thai lunch. Afternoon relaxing at the lake. Guided kayak tour. Dinner at the Raft House. Night Safari on the lake.

Morning: Kayaking, then morning meal at the raft house. Trekking through the jungle to a cave and a small lake with a guide. Lunch and relaxing at the lake and return to Khao Lak.

4 days / 3 nights Khao Sok / Cheow Lan Lake

Elephant Hills offers 3 or 4-day trips that they combine with the activities with the elephants in their camp. Always included is the contact with elephants is always included, in this case it is feeding and washing them. A real experience!

One night you sleep by the Khao Sok Park in a luxury tent in the rain forest, the other nights in a luxury tent on a raft on Cheow Lan Lake. You can go trekking over a hill with a guide and visit a stalactite cave or kayak by yourself or with a guide on the lake.

Massage

Thai massages are world famous and hardly any hotel opens in Khao Lak today that does not have "Spa" in its name.

However, you cannot only get the massages at the hotel spa, but also on the beach. The advantage is a very low price. The disadvantages are: the quality is very dependent on the person that does the massage. How good are their skills? Even in the shade it can get very hot on the beach. You do not only sweat yourself; it is very tiring for the massaging person. For your own protection, have a look at the pad you lie on and possibly lay your own towel on it. On the beach you are massaged through the bathing suit, which can be an obstacle.

Another possibility are massage parlors, which can also be found in Khao Lak. The massages there are a step (or maybe more, depending on the place) above the beach ... they can get as good as a really good hotel spa massage.

In Phuket / Patong we have often visited the Let's Relax, a place I highly recommend. I have also never been proposed to have a "happy ending" there ... which sometimes still can occur, depending on the site. (Though less in Khao Lak, I think). In Khao Lak I prefer the hotel spa.

Here is a **description of a spa visit** (in case you want to try it).

You start at the reception with a cold towel (it is hot outside) and a refreshing green tea drink.

Then you proceed into the spa area. There is a private room with an anteroom, where you can change: undress to your underwear (take off the bra), maybe use the hygienically packed uni-size net underpants and put on the provided bathrobe and slippers.

Before starting the massage you get a footbath and a foot scrub, and the person massaging you will also explain what the procedure and ask for your preferences.

Then you lie on the massage table (in massage parlors, you are often massaged while on the floor on a mat),first on the stomach, then on the back.

Thai massages are usually done through clothes or a towel and without oil, but there are of course mixed massages, or you can choose an aromatherapy or Swedish massage. The body parts that are not massaged are always covered, so you do not get cold. The rooms are air-conditioned.

During the massage, you look at a pretty flower arrangement on the floor, listen to soothing music and just enjoy it. I regularly manage to doze off for a while, but for my wife the massage is usually too ... energ(et)ic.

Upon completion and clothing again, you finish with a sweet-sharp ginger tea.

At the Tailor

In Khao Lak there are many tailors, 30 at the last count. Some of them have started with a tactic that has been in use in Patong for a few years: they are waiting on the road in front of the shop and talk to everyone in hope that somebody enters. I do not like that particularly, but on the other side, visiting to a tailor actually is something you should do once when you are in Thailand.

Therefore, I compiled **a small guide** for it:

Even if the tailors like to have you in their shop to convince you, it is better to come somewhat prepared, to have a plan of what you want or how much you want to spend. There are several options: You can have favorite clothes that no longer fit changed. You can recreate your favorite dress, trousers or shirt from a different cloth (or length, etc.). Take it with you to show. Or you can have made something completely new. Templates can be obtained from magazines; they have a lot of visual material in the shop.

You can choose from the (many) cloth samples in the store. If the tailor does not have the desired one in stock, they can often get it from other stores. – Obviously these "many" tailor shops often have the same owners ...

Experience says that it is good idea to listen to the recommendations for the cloth. Not every material is suitable for any type of clothing. I was always satisfied with the recommended cloth – even in terms of durability. There are silk fabrics that can be washed easily and my wife used them for years.

After selecting the piece of clothing and material you are measured.

The price is a not an easy topic. I can only recommend to negotiate ... The first prize I was normally told was on the same level as a similar purchase in Switzerland ... and that is (too) high for Thailand, even if the dress is tailored. Negotiate and ask for a quantity discount (if you can order 3 of the same shirts) you should get a fair price.

Agree on everything in writing and make an appointment in a few days (at least 2), after which you go back to the tailor for the fitting.

The clothes are still held together pretty temporarily during the fitting and the tailor notes the changes that are to be made with his chalk. You make the next appointment (again in 2 days or so) when you can then hopefully try the finished product.

If something does not fit right or needs to be changed, you have to come back again. Usually it fits. You pay (mostly by credit card) and take your custom made clothes home.

Please note: there are customs regulations for the import of products from a different country: maybe you have to pay VAT.

(If you do not, at least they do not take your clothes away as they do with fake brand clothes).

Phuket

Phuket Excursions: Many tour operators offer day trips to Phuket, often you can put a tour together yourself. Here are a few recommendations for what to see and do.

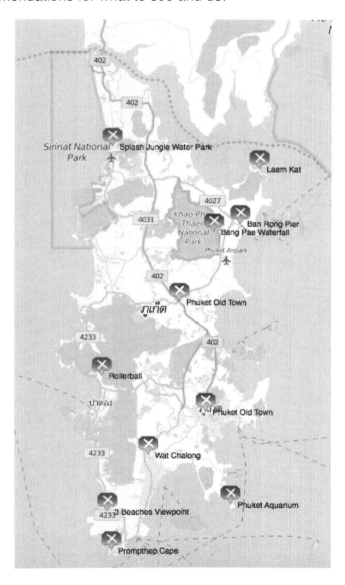

Sarasin Bridge

Phuket is an island. Technically. But because it is so large you often do not feel to be on an island when there. Phuket is separated from the mainland by water. However, these are just about 500 meters of water and there is a bridge connecting the two parts of the country. Meanwhile, there have actually been three bridges in the same place. The first bridge was built in 1967 and was named Sarasin after a now forgotten local politician. Before that, there was a ferry on the site. Because traffic (and increasing tourism) in the 70s was too much for the first small bridge, a second bridge was built there in the 80s. And then 2011 came the newest version. This one is called Thepkasattri Bridge, but most people actually still talk of the Sarasin Bridge. The old bridge (the 2nd) still is there and was provided with a pretty building on it – today it is regarded as a minor tourist attraction that can be walked on by foot.

DG 8.20165 98.29795
GMS   N 8° 12' 5.94"   O 98° 17' 52.62"

It is especially nice to view the sunset from the small platform in the middle of the second bridge. In the evening, anglers can be seen next to the tourists. On the Phuket side there are small stalls with drinks and food.

On the Phang Nga side there are a number of popular small stores where you can buy dried fish, T-shirts and toys. Here is also the best parking option for a visit to the bridge.

Phuket Waterpark – Splash Jungle

This is something for those who do not have enough water in the hotel swimming pool, the sea, the waterfalls and perhaps Cheow Lan Lake: The colorful water park has a variety of exciting water slides such as the Boomerango, and the Super Bowl, a wave pool, a lazy river where you can drift, and a water playground for children and restaurant / bars

Open 10 am - 6 pm
Location: Close to the Airport Phuket. At the Centara Grand.

DG 8.11748 98.3062
GMS   N 8° 7' 2.928"   O 98° 18' 22.32"

Entrance: about 1300 baht for adults and 650 baht for children (up to 12 years). It is free for children below 5 years.

North-east Phuket

A self-drive trip with views of the Phang Nga Bay, non-tourist areas, a floating restaurant and more.

Phuket has become very touristy and overcrowded. The last time when we were driving around there, I got the feeling that there are more cars on the road than residents. All the more surprisingly, there are still off the beaten track areas and routes left to discover almost untouched spots by tourists. If you want to see a bit from the Phuket of earlier times, you should make this trip.

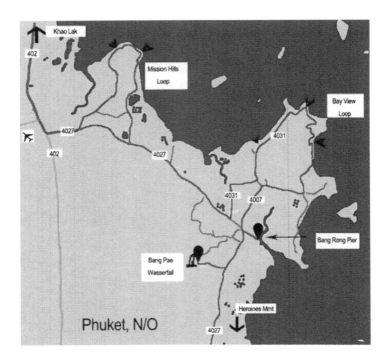

In the northeast of Phuket are two "loops": roads that make a big detour to return to the main path ... in this case the main path itself is more a side road.

There are two ways to get there and **to Laem Khat:** Driving in from the south or the north.:

From the south: take the 4027 at the roundabout at the Heroines Monument and turn off towards **Ao Po Pier** and after 12 km turn right. After about 3 km take the motorway (turn to the right) to "Radi Medical Center" (there is a sign). Follow the road and you get on a pretty loop that brings you to secluded beaches, stunning views of the cliffs and islands in Phang Nga Bay on some steep curves and a roller coaster-like elevation change and then back to Ao Po Road.

DG 8.09804 98.43248
GMS   N 8° 5' 52.944"   O 98° 25' 56.927"

Even more beautiful views, but a less spectacular road can be found at the **Mission Hills Loop** just next to it.

DG 8.11624 98.37381
GMS N 8° 6' 58.464"O 98° 22' 25.716"

To get there (this time from the north): from the Thepkasatri Road (this is Highway 402, the main connection axis in the center of Phuket and the road that leads over the bridge to the mainland) take off to the left into the small side road 4027 just south of the junction to the airport. Take care; the entrance to the road is narrow, you see it very late and it is missed easily. This is awkward because the road there (as is often the case in Phuket) is divided into two parts by a non-crossable middle lane and you have to drive on to the next U-turn (3 km), where you can turn, go back to the airport junction with the traffic lights, where you again cannot turn right, so you have to drive into the road to the airport (to the left) and then make another U-turn there to return to the junction with the traffic lights and then finally take a second attempt to catch the road ...

Road 4027 (if one has managed to get onto) is a well-paved road and the further you get, the less traveled. Take the road to Baan Laem Srai (to the left) for the good views at the bay. At the end of the loop you get out at the Mission Hills Golf Course.

If you continue to follow road 4027 further, you get to the back entrance of the above described loop: look for the sign for Radi Medical Center, which you follow.

There are big pineapple plantations and palm trees and rubber are grown around here.

Bang Rong Pier

The area is a Muslim community, so you can see veiled women and men in Muslim clothing on their daily chores.

The road to the pier is easy to find. From road 4027 turn off at the mosque and follow the signs to Bang Rong Pier.

DG 8.0498   98.41583
GMS   N 8° 2' 59.28"   O 98° 24' 56.987"

There is an entry gate – if you park here for a long time (for example to take the ferry to Koh Yao Noi), then you have to pay. But if you only come to see the place and have something to eat, parking is free. **Monkeys** can often be seen in the mangroves next to the road – they can be a bit cheeky, so be careful.

The pier is often a hive of activity, not only because of the ferry, but there are also fishing boats of the locals (large and small) and some cargo transport that is made over the waterway.

If you turn left at the waterfront and follow the wooden boardwalk through the mangroves, you soon reach **a floating restaurant**. Although the small local restaurant has few tourists, they do have a menu in English available, and the food is good and very cheap. You cannot get alcohol there, but fresh juices and other beverages are sold. During the meal you can watch the activity on the water and observe birds and fish.

From here you can make **boat trips by kayak into the mangroves** – just ask at the restaurant.

Phuket Gibbon Rehabilitation Project und Bang Pae Waterfall

Gibbons are endangered long-armed monkeys, which are unfortunately often misused to extract money from tourists, by for example offering to have a picture taken with them. Some are also kept as pets. This is illegal and captive gibbons have a miserable life – when they get older and more aggressive they become useless for the owners.

The gibbons which are taken away from their owners by the police, get a second chance at the Gibbon Rehabilitation Project. They go through a long period of rehabilitation before attempts are made to release them into the woods again. This does not work with all the animals.

You are informed about the various gibbons and their stories on posters. The Gibbons are in large cages, some silent, some making their typical call, some climbing around.

If you are offered to take a picture with a gibbon in Phuket or somewhere else in Thailand, take a picture of the owner and email it with the information where it was taken to this project: grp@gibbonproject.org. You can also support them with a donation on the project sit. By the way: the organization does not get any money from the park entry fees here (200 Baht).

DG 8.04242 98.39326
GMS   N 8° 2' 32.712"   O 98° 23' 35.735"

A little further back, the road leads to the Bang Pae Waterfall. At the restaurant near the car park you can stock up on drinks before you go, but please take the bottles back again. The narrow footpath leads over an up-and-down (but mostly up) up to a relatively small waterfall in a mini-canyon.

Heroines Monument

A monument, that you will almost certainly see when you are visiting Phuket. It is dedicated to the two sisters Muk and Chan, who led the local population defending against an attack by the Burmese and managed to repel them. The monument is located in the center of the island on the main axis between north and south – smack in the middle of a roundabout. You can see it well from the car, but on foot you have a real problem if you want to cross the road – especially with today's traffic.

DG 7.98097 98.36391
GMS   N 7° 58' 51.492" O 98° 21' 50.076"

Phuket Town

Phuket Town was built at the time of the tin mining, when the island benefitted from a great financial boost. In **the old town** of Phuket you can see spacious Sino-Colonial buildings built about 100 years ago. The quarter can be easily explored on foot. Five streets contain most points of interest: **Thalang Road**, one of the oldest streets, lined with many boutique shops and restaurants in its historic buildings today, **Radada Road**, **Phang Nga Road**, **Dibuk Road** and **Krabi Road** and the narrow streets (Sois) around them.

The big **On On Hotel** is well known. It is the oldest hotel in Phuket, (opened 1929) and was also seen in the movie "The Beach" starring Leonardo Di Caprio. In 2012 it was completely refurbished. Today it is called "Memory" and is no longer looking shabby.
DG 7.88513 98.38646
GMS N 7 ° 53 '6.468' 'O 98 ° 23' 11,255 "

Further in the old town: the Chinese temple **Jui Tui Shrine**. Location: on Soi Phuthorn, Ranong Road. The temple has been renovated several times and is colorful and well worth seeing.

Walking Street: A market takes place at the weekend, 4 pm to 10 pm.

Phuket Trickeye Museum is interesting for children. Opened in 2014, it is purely devoted to optical illusions. You can stand in the (100) perspectival painted pictures and take amazing and amusing photos of yourself. The museum is located at the intersection of Montri and Phang Nga Road. Opening times 9 am - 9 pm.
DG 7.88317 98.3925
GMS   N 7° 52' 59.412" O 98° 23' 32.999"

Phuket Aquarium

A visit to this aquarium makes a nice afternoon trip with the family where you learn something about life in the sea. Hundreds of colorful exotic fish and other sea creatures can be seen in the 30 tanks here including an underwater tunnel between sharks, manta rays and other large fish. I do not know whether the open tank where you could also touch marine creatures such as sea cucumbers, starfish and sea urchins is still there – but that was Junior's favorite.

Open 8.30 am to 4 pm, 7 days a week.

Admission: Adults 100 Baht, Children 50 Baht

DG 7.80347 98.40788
GMS   N 7° 48' 12.492" O 98° 24' 28.368"

Wat Chalong

Also called Chaithararam temple. The most important temple on Phuket and one of the largest and most prestigious in the area.

Magical powers are attributed to one of the revered monks here and many people come here to ask for help – if their desire is fulfilled, they burn chains of fireworks ... which often happens.

The newest building there is the large Chedi, which you can climb up inside under the tip.

Opening times daily from 7 am to 5 pm.

Directions: Coming from the roundabout in Chalong after about 4 km on the right side. Coming from Central Festival after about 6 km on the left side.

DG 7.84678 98.3369
GMS   N 7° 50' 48.408" O 98° 20' 12.839"

At the time **around the Chinese New Year** (2017 this will be on the 28th January) **the big market takes place at the Wat Chalong**. There you cannot only shop and try the diverse food, but you can also use the simple fun rides.

Promthep Cape

The southernmost point of Phuket is a very popular destination, especially for sunset. Despite ample parking, it can get very crowded then. It is a nice place for the sunset ... but to be fair this is great elsewhere on the coast as well.

The point offers **a view** to Naiharn, to the Racha Islands and other small islands in the Andaman Sea, but I always found the (ever changing) **huge collection of elephant statues** most interesting.

Laem Promthep can be approached from both Nau Harn and from Rawai.

Opening times: around the clock – before 5 pm there are way less people.

DG 7.76321 98.3052
GMS   N 7° 45' 47.556" O 98° 18' 18.719"

Karon (Kata) Viewpoint: 3-Beaches Viewpoint

One of the most famous views of Phuket. You can see the beaches Kata Noim, Kata Yai and Karon (in that order) and in the sea off Kata Beach the island of Ko Pu.

Directions: Coming from Kata up on the way towards Kata Noi, turn left up the steep hill. Coming from Van Chalong, Rawai, Nai Harn there is an intersection in Saiyuan where you can choose to go to Nai Harn, Chalong and Kata. Follow the road towards Kata.

Opening times: around the clock

DG 7.79722 98.30226
GMS   N 7° 47' 49.992" O 98° 18' 8.136"

Patong Zorbing

Stepping into a large, padded, translucent plastic ball and rolling down a slope in it is called Zorbing or Roller Ball. Zorbing was invented in New Zealand, but there are now a number of places where you can do it – as here in Phuket.

In Kalim, just north of Patong, on the hilltop you have a nice view over Patong and can also enjoy a drink, if you do not want to try Zorbing.

Equipped with la life vest you step into the ball and get some fresh water poured in (which is good, because of the temperatures and because the water helps you slide inside when the ball is rolling ... so that you do not somersault like a hamster in the too-fast turning wheel). You can choose between 2 tracks: the straight one is steeper and looks a little scary, but it is actually the easier one. Rolling down the curvy track feels like being on a waterslide where you cannot really see where you are going ... and are tossed around. At the end of the tracks you will be safely stopped by a net-wall and are transported back up by car.

What to bring: swimsuit, some courage

Cost: from 950 baht per person and "ride" and 1 drink, up to 1950 baht for 6 rides, drink, snack, T-shirt and photo. Open: 10 am – 6 pm

Location: Kalim Bay View, Patong (well signed)
DG 7.91683 98.29714
GMS   N 7° 55' 0.588"   O 98° 17' 49.703"

More Things To Do and See On Phuket

Butterfly Garden – nice, but I recommend visiting the one up in Khao Lak.

Phuket Zoo – I strongly advise against a visit here. The zoo has already been several times in the media for animal cruelty ... and the animal pens look really dreary.

Tiger Kingdom – a newer attraction where visitors can have their pictures taken with living tigers of different ages (at your own risk and under supervision). I do not know how animal friendly that is, but when I think of the controversy with the Tiger Temple in Ayutthaya in northern Thailand ... I wouldn't recommend it.

Phuket Wake Park: water park with possibilities to surf cable wakeboards and standing waves. Something for older children.

Patong Beach – Known for its nightlife (no longer as extreme as it used to be, since they have monitored closing times) and shopping.

Big Buddha – exactly what it sounds like: a big Buddha, on a hill in the middle of Phuket, with a view.

Simon Cabaret Show with transvestites – Now there is a similar (smaller) show in Khao Lak as well.

Shopping malls and outlet stores – Mostly Asian-inspired products and home furnishings etc.

Gems Gallery – Jewelry and jewels of good quality and with warranty. The prices are accordingly.

There is much more to see and do: archery shooting, go-karting, monkey and snake shows, climbing parks ... but there are also good guide books focusing on Phuket.

Occasionally you also are offered **trips to Phi Phi Island** in Khao Lak. The island is located further south than Phuket and although day trips are possible – I think it is too much of a hassle for what you can see in such a short time. The last time I was there was almost 10 years ago, and even then I thought it was an artificial hype ... and I was kind of disappointed by the corals that suffer by the many tourists and the boats. I do not think that has improved since.

You can book day trips at a lot of places and not driving yourself on Phuket can take a lot of the stress away. The guides are often very flexible concerning planning and which places to see – especially when it comes to small groups.

Overview Map

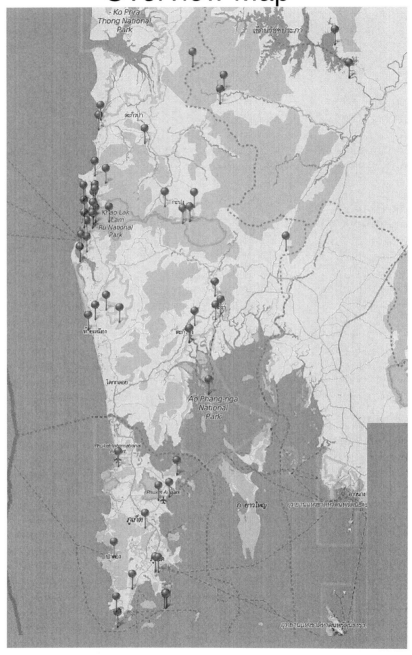

What For Who? Tips For Everyone

Tips For Families With Children:

Build the biggest sand castle on the beach
Phang Nga Bay Tour
Waterfall with fish: in the Sri Phang Nga Park
Khao Sok tours and activities
Elephant riding
Bamboo Raft rides
Kayaking: in the mangroves on river or lake
Khao Lak Mini Golf
Turtle Conservatory
Snorkeling trip Ko Tachai
Water Park Phuket
Phuket Trickeye Museum
Phuket Aquarium

Tips For Couples

Stroll on the beach in the evening
Romantic dinner on the beach
Sunset dinner on a Chinese junk in Phang Nga Bay
Book a massage
Take a bath with the Elephant
Bamboo raft ride in the green rainforest
Moo Moo's Cabaret
Let a sky lantern fly at night
Have new clothes made at the tailor
Eat cakes or crepes or ice in the Cafe Kantary
Snorkeling trip Similan Islands
Cheow Lan Lake: stay the night on the water

Tips for Self Driving: Routes of Half-Day and Day Tours).

Temples and caves tour Phang Nga:

Khao Lak (Temple) – Phang NGA Wat Suwan Khuha – Phung Chang Cave – Wat Thamtapan – Sa Nang Manora Forest Ntl Park – Khao Lak

Kapong Tour – nature and culture:

Khao Lak – Lam Ru Waterfall, – Kapong Temple – hot springs – Takua Pa Old Town – Khao Lak

Everything Water:

Khao Lak – Sau Rung Waterfall – Ban Bam Khem Tsunami Memorial Center – ferry to Ko Kho Khao, ferry back – Tam Nang Waterfall – Khao Lak

Phuket, the North:

Khao Lak – Sarasin Bridge – Mission Hills Loop – Laem Loop – lunch at the floating restaurant at Bang Rong Pier – Gibbons Rehabilitation Project and Bang Pae Waterfall – Heroines Monument – Khao Lak

Phuket completely:

Khao Lak – Sarasin Bridge – Heroines Monument – Phuket Town – Wat Chalong – Promthrep Cape – 3 Beaches View Point – return via the beach resorts: Kata – Karon – Patong – Kamala coastal road – Heroines Monument – return to Khao Lak. (Note: due to heavy traffic on Phuket this is really a day trip and self-drive rather tiring).

Do's and Don'ts in Thailand

Respect for the royal family: never insult the king who is highly revered. (And do not destroy money with his image).

Respect for Buddha: do not climb on Buddha statues, do not buy and export Buddha statues or images either.

The soles of the feet should never be turned towards someone, as this is considered to be very rude.

Thais should **never be touched on the head** (not even kids!), since the soul is located there.

The left hand is considered unclean (that is also the one you use to wash yourself on the toilet), so if you hand someone money / a gift / some food always do that with the right hand.

Touching in public or openly **showing physical contact** (except for hand-holding) is not welcome.

Be mindful of Monks. Some are not allowed to touch women. As a woman you therefore ask a man to give the alms, or put them on the floor.

The Wai is the Thai greeting. It is not expected of a foreigner to return it, especially since it is not easy to carry it out properly with all its deeper meanings. How low the head is bowed or the hands lifted depends on your own status and that of the person opposite. It is safer for a tourist to just smile and nod.

Thais usually address each other with the **first name** – which means that your own transfer or tour reservations are occasionally not found if you only look for your family name.

Thais talk to each other mainly with nicknames, which they often receive as babies.

Occasionally you will be asked **personal questions** that seem almost indiscreet. A typical question would be "How much you earn?" – This is pure sympathy and curiosity. You can answer it well with something like: "I do not know myself," or "It's enough for us"...

Gräng Jai describes a typical Thai trait and means: be considerate of others, do not make any claims, show restraint. Mutual sympathy and a polite approach are very important. Many Thais therefore also do not like to say "No" if a positive reply is expected – just not to disappoint.

Confrontations are avoided, so that both sides do not lose their face. Therefore, one should also not publicly renounce the country and criticize people. If you really have to criticize, remain friendly and balance it with praise and ... smile a lot.

Thus in Thailand **a smile opens doors** ... a smile helps you to get over so many (of your own) mistakes.

Eating in Thailand

Thai food is a mix of Chinese, Indian and European influences that have merged over time to its own national cuisine. Thai food is tasty and does not make you fat. There is a lot of rice – actually the Thai expression for "have a meal" literally means "eat rice" ... but the additions and spices make the food so tasty.

Kaeng – these are different "Curry"-dishes. However, they do not contain curry powder but are made with a spice paste as a base. Galangal or ginger with kefir lime leaves are used for this paste, along with fresh chilies and shrimp paste, which are all mashed in a mortar until a homogeneous paste is formed. There are red and green Kaeng dishes with different types of meat or fish or tofu.

Tom Kha Kai – chicken soup with coconut milk, spicy-sweet, with galangal, lemongrass, chili and coconut milk, which soothes some of the spiciness. Tom Kha Kai is also a Kaeng dish and definitely a favorite food of mine, which can also be enjoyed if not so spicy. Instead of chicken it may contain seafood and the vegetables vary depending on the cook.

Tom Yam – hot and sour shrimp soup: spicy and hot. With fish sauce, shallots, lemongrass, lime juice, galangal, tamarind and chilli. Classically with shrimp, but there are also versions with other fish and seafood.

Phat Thai – noodles with vegetables and meat, the national dish of Thailand. This is a one-plate meal that combines the four flavors: hot, sour, salty and sweet. It contains dried chilies, lime, fish sauce and cane sugar ... The noodles are fried with egg, tofu and small, dried shrimp. bean sprouts, chives and chopped roasted peanuts are served with it – often separately.

Phat Kaphrao – a single-plate meal with minced meat (pork or chicken or beef, but also shrimp) with Thai basil – the more pungent and aromatic version of the one known here. Chili, garlic and soy sauce are added, all fried in a wok and served with rice.

Satay skewers – This dish originates from Indonesia or Malaysia. These are skewers of grilled spiced meat, served with a sauce. The meat on the skewers is mostly chicken, but can also be fish or beef or pork. However – the spice mixture always contains turmeric, which gives it the typical yellow color. It is frequently served with a peanut sauce dip.

Som Tam – papaya salad (spicy), a kind of salad made with chopped and mashed green (unripe) papaya, onions, tomatoes. With lime, long beans, roasted peanuts, salt, palm sugar and chilli, seasoned with fish sauce. Shrimp are often included (mostly dried, sometimes also fresh). It is usually very spicy (!) and slightly tart.

Tempura – vegetables and shrimp fried in a light batter. The dish originates from Japan or India and contains various vegetables (small corncob, onion rings, beans, papaya) or shrimp or fish that is cut into pieces and freshly dipped in a light batter and then deep-fried.

Squid with pepper and garlic sauce – This dish can be ordered in the simplest local Thai restaurants and consists of various kinds of meat, fish or squid with a sauce of dark roasted garlic and pepper, served with rice.

Table manners

Originally Thai food was eaten with the fingers – which is still the case in some regions today and with some dishes. But today you normally use fork and spoon. Most of the time there are no knifes and you will not need any because the food has been prepared in bite-sized pieces. The fork is used to slide something onto the spoon – the spoon then goes to the mouth.

Chopsticks are not part of Thai cuisine and are only used in Chinese restaurants or to eat Chinese and Vietnamese noodle dishes. Then you hold the spoon in the left hand and the chopsticks in the right.

Toilets

While the toilets found in the hotels are almost exclusively Western-style toilets, the ones outside are usually not. Therefore you may encounter such thud-loos in restaurants, gas stations, and shops or in smaller lodging. And there may be no toilet paper.

Do not panic, you will still get clean – the Thais just use another system. As a beginner, it is advisable to entirely take off your clothes below the waistline to prevent accidents. With some practice you can later kept your pants / skirt / underpants on and just strip them down far, but at the beginning it is really better to take them off. Then crouch over the hole (facing the door, knees towards the ceiling) and let go. Physiologically this is a better position than sitting on the loo, even if it is very unusual for us.

After business wash yourself with the (left!) hand and water. The water either comes from a hose or bucket with a ladle which you can find in every Thai toilet. With the right hand draw/spray the water, with the left one clean thoroughly. Provided you use enough water, this is not a grisly affair. Rinse the toilet well with the water as you finish.

If there is toilet paper – or if you brought some – use it to dry yourself. The toilets are not designed to flush the paper though – there is a bin, where you can dispose of it. Although 1-2 leaves usually go down, do not try to flush more!

Then thoroughly wash your hands and get dressed – that is it.

Electricity

Thailand uses **sockets** (and plugs) of the types A, B, C. Older outlets are Type A, modern outlets are a combination of types B and C. They can accept the American plug types A and B and the Europlug C.

This means you can use the (two-pole) plugs from Switzerland or Germany in the newer systems without adapters.

The **main voltage in Thailand is 230 Volts** as it is in Europe – so you can use your electric devices without problems in Thailand, because the deviation is still within the tolerance range of the electrical equipment. For tourists from the USA, where they use 120 Volts – there may be problems or you need a converter. Have a look at the chargers for laptops, tablets, smartphones, cameras. If it says INPUT: 100-240 Volt, 50/60 Hz – that means that these devices can be used in the specified line voltage range around the world – also in Thailand.

Noteworthy here are the **myriads of cables** you see hanging everywhere, and so also unfortunately in front of the most beautiful sights in Thailand. Unlike Europe, where the power supply of houses is carried out largely underground, the electrical cables in Thailand hang above the ground on poles. Every house seems to have at least one cable going to the mast. To save costs, the homeowners in many regions are allowed to put up power cables themselves. So you can frequently see entire families working together to hang the cables from large cable drums onto existing poles. Safety is often disregarded – and occasionally accidents occur when a pole is under current. In the country side power outages occur when the network is overloaded.

Telephone, Roaming, Internet

Thailand is not a third world country concerning mobile phones. Many Thais sport the latest phone models and the connection is good almost everywhere (the only exception is in the midst of the Khao Sok National Park at the northern end of Cheow Lan Lake).

However, for most foreigners it is not a good idea to use your phone with the SIM card from home to make calls or use the Internet, because you may quickly accumulate high bills due to the expensive roaming charges. Just once I had to use my (Swiss) phone to look up something on Facebook and Google ... and after just 5 minutes I got a warning message that my credit for the month had already been used up.

You best get a Thai **SIM card** right after arriving in Thailand. For example one by one2call, TrueMove or DTAC – you can buy them on every corner (even at the airport) for about 50 Baht. Using the card is simple: place it in the cell phone and activate it via the number stated on the packaging of the card. Then you load credit onto the card. This is possible in every 7-Eleven store (or alternatively online).

To call home use the cheap call-numbers: 007, 008 and 009 – For England like this: 009 44 followed by the area code without the zeros.. etc. or for the USA 009 1...

For Switzerland (country code 41), Basel (area code 061) it would be: 009 41 61 XXX XX XX)

Internet:

There are still some Internet cafes around – also in Khao Lak, but the computers suffer from the high humidity and must be replaced frequently, which makes it here minimally more expensive than elsewhere. In addition, these public computers are sometimes painfully slow. In the hotel there are often public computers that you can use to connect to the Internet, or they offer Wi-fi.

Wi-fi access is now available in most hotels and free for guests – you often must register for access at the reception and ask for the password.

On the other hand you can then even surf in the Internet on the beach.

Withdrawing Money

You do not need to change money at home, as you can get it easily in Thailand. There are **Exchange Offices** in the airport, but they are said to offer a worse exchange rate than the ones outside in the streets.

Pretty much all the major **banks** of Thailand have now **a branch in Khao Lak**. Most of them are located in the center (La On), only TMB is in Bang Niang.

In addition to the counters, they also have **ATM machines** where you can withdraw money with your Visa, MasterCard and Maestro cards. The TBank (orange) supposedly has the best exchange rates, however looking around worth it.

The ATMs give out 1000 baht notes and in Khao Lak you have the opportunity to set the language to English – which makes sense, since it is somewhat difficult to read Thai.

One characteristic the ATMs here have, unlike those at home, is that once you have chosen how much money you withdraw, you receive it from the machine, THEN the question concerning receipt follows and only AFTER THAT your card comes out. This has already led us once to leave without the card. Luckily it was very early in the morning and the machine pulls the card in after about a minute. We could even retrieve it from the bank with some local assistance.

Hotels also exchange money, but usually at a worse rate – but they are open after 9 pm.

Health

It is worth visiting the pharmacy prior to a trip to obtain advice and information. You can also look up a lot of info on sites like www.safetravel.ch (in German) or http://wwwnc.cdc.gov/travel (in English).

Khao Lak with its warm and humid climate poses some health risks that are not that known in our areas, such as:

Sunburns:

Use Sunscreen. This is especially important here because of the proximity to the equator. Sunburn is not only acutely uncomfortable, but may have long-term effects - it promotes the development of skin cancer.

For Thais, white skin is still an ideal of beauty ... and they do not understand the tanning craze of the Europeans. They protect themselves from the sun with long-sleeved clothing, hats and umbrellas. And you will find in most personal care product in Asia some skin-bleaching agent (even in deodorant!).

Gastrointestinal problems:

Although we have never had problems in Thailand even if we ate at night markets and in very small local stalls, this needs to be mentioned. The most common cause of gastrointestinal complaints is bad, raw or inadequately cooked food. The water that comes out of the tap in Khao Lak is not drinkable, but can be used for brushing teeth (although some hotels also provide extra water) for this.

Melons appear to be problematic (also in fruit shakes and fruit salads) if they are cut open and left lying around for too long. Meat should be well done. If you can select your fish/seafood yourself, make sure that the eyes are clear and not sunken in.

Elephant-mites:

These mites can be transmitted to humans by poorly maintained and affected elephants. That is why you should not sit on the elephant with bare skin ... and perhaps have a look at the legs of the mahouts before you get on. The mites cause scabies-like symptoms (skin red, itchy, scaly, especially in the folds), but are harmless and they die soon since man is an accidental host. Do not scratch the skin, as this can lead to infection.

Mosquito bites and mosquito-transmitted diseases:

Mosquitos especially come out at dusk, but some species also bite during the day, so always use strong mosquito repellent, possibly local products, if they are already immune to the one you have. The bites should not be scratched, because that leads to infections and outright holes in the skin.

Chikungunya fever: This is a mosquito-transmitted viral disease appearing in southern Thailand. The symptoms are high fever with joint pain and tenderness. After 1-2 weeks most get well by themselves again, but occasionally permanent joint problems remain.

Dengue: This is also a mosquito-transmitted viral infection. It has non-specific symptoms such as head-, joint- and limb-pain, fever, occasionally a rash. In some cases it takes a more serious course with bleeding complications and derailment of blood pressure. In that case it is potentially life threatening and must be treated in a hospital.

Malaria: With this mosquito-transmitted disease there is no problem in Khao Lak. Introduced cases of the mosquito-borne disease come from northern Thailand.

Zika: there have been some individual cases in Thailand, so pregnant women (or those who want to get pregnant shortly) are advised to use precaution and talk to their doctor.

Other Health Hazards:

Unrestrained (wild) **dogs** should not be fed or caressed. Hookworms can frolic in their fur and with the dog droppings, these hookworms get into sand, so you had better not walk barefoot on beaches with dogs. The minute worms penetrate the body over the skin and migrate to the lungs via the blood, as larvae they are coughed up and swallowed, and the adult worm in the intestine sucks blood form its host. Because of the loss of blood, long after returning home you get anemia, fatigue, depression and stomach problems. If hookworms are suspected, a doctor should be consulted and an an anthelmintic prescribed.

Monkeys can bite pretty badly (as dogs and cats) and the wounds often become infected. A visit to a doctor is absolutely necessary. You Also should be vaccinated against tetanus and possibly rabies after a bite. It is definitely best to avoid any contact.

Jellyfish are occasionally to be found in the water. Most are so small that you cannot even see them and only feel when you have been stung. They are annoying, but usually not dangerous. Rarely there may be poisonous jellyfish, if the slightest touch can leave severe pain, skin rashes and even scarring. Portuguese Man and Box Jellyfish are the most dangerous. But these are visible and you should stay away. Upon contact, it helps to pour highly concentrated vinegar over it (maybe take some from home, you cannot get it there), wash it with water and go to the doctor if no improvement occurs. Thais use a paste of the green Vine with the violet flowers which can often be found on the beach to treat jellyfish stings.

Sea urchins are found primarily on the (large) rocks in the water. Whoever steps on one gets the thin spikes in the sole of the foot, where they can break off and cause severe pain. A doctor should remove the spines – or, if none is available, you can try to use a paste of Papaya: its enzyme papain softens the skin, so the spines come out by themselves the next day.

Ever since Steve Irwin died of a **stingray** sting people know how dangerous they can be. A sting leads to severe pain and being stung in the abdomen and face is dangerous. Pakarang Beach is known to have stingrays, so it is advisable there to go in the water only with caution and slippers.

Swimming, snorkeling and scuba diving is great, but one principle applies here as elsewhere: nothing in the sea should be touched. For nature's and also for your own safety.

In lakes and ponds small parasites causing **schistosomiasis** live. They come into the water with human feces. where the larvae enter through the skin an itchy rash develops, and later you may develop an acute febrile illness with possible organ involvement, which can be dangerous. A physician should be consulted in case of symptoms. With early treatment the prognosis is good.

This may all sound a bit disconcerting, but in all the years we went there we did not experience any of these problems – except for the small harmless jellyfish in the sea and mosquitoes in the evening. We have almost eaten everywhere, have been in a lot of water (flowing and standing) and have not suffered from any negative consequences.

Caution is always important: Stay away from animals, eat where the Thais eat and protect yourself against mosquito bites – then not much can happen.

Doctors and Pharmacies

Those who get sick in Khao Lak have several doctors to choose from. Some of them also make hotel-visits.

Dr. Chusak – He is a pediatrician and general practitioner working in the Takua Pa Hospital during daytime. In his small clinic in Khao Lak he also treats adult patients. He also makes home visits – he is the doctor we needed once on Ko Kho Khao. Location: Ban La On opposite the Jai Restaurant. Opening hours: 5.30pm to 8.30 pm. Tel (076) 48 57 38 or (081) 9689701 (prefix for Thailand: +66)

Dr. Amaornrut (Mrs.) has a practice in Bang Niang on the main road between Tonys Lodge and the Motive Cottage Resort. Her Clinic is open daily from 3 pm to 8.30 pm. Tel Tel: (083) 647 7053

Dr. Seree which is mentioned in some guides is now retired and living in Takua Pa.

In many small towns there are first aid stations and small clinics – also in Khao Lak. However, the equipment and hygienic conditions are not up to European standards and as a tourist you will therefore quickly be brought in a larger hospital, such as in Takua Pa, or Phuket – where there are several hospitals that are also very well equipped.

Clinik Dr. Sumet in Bang Niang with opening times from 10.30 am to 4.30 pm Wed-Thu and Fri-Sat: 1 pm – 8 pm. (086) 946-76-38.

Inter Clinic: Bang Niang Beach Road. Opening times 9 am – 9 pm daily Tel (076) 48 65 51 and (087) 628 35 77

Takuapa Hospital: 39/2 Moo 1 T. Bang Naisri, Takua Pa, Tel +66 (0) 79 431 488

Ambulance in Bang Niang: 1719

If you have an accident on the road (for example as a motorcyclist) you are taken to hospital by one of the many private ambulances. In very remote areas probably a few helpful Thais just put you in the back of the car and bring you there.

Decompression chambers are needed in diving accidents. In Khao Lak, thanks to caring dive guides, they apparently have never had a fatal accident. There is a first aid station at Khuk Khak, but the nearest decompression chamber is located on Phuket: the Phuket International Hospital in Phuket Town.

SSS Network / Khao Lak, Khuk Khak, opening times: 9 am to 6 pm / 24 hrs. Emergency: +66 (0) 6 283 1941 or +66 (0) 9 871 4302

Medical treatments are usually cheaper in Thailand than in Europe, and therefore in some areas health tourism has developed, especially for Dental treatments. Many dentists on Phuket have adapted to foreign patients, speak English and have international standards.

Dentists in Khao Lak:

Dental Home 21/20 Moo 7, Petchkasem Road – Tel.: (0) 76485-895

Dental Clinic 5/55 Moo 7, Petchkasem Road (in Book Trees complex) Tel.: (0) 88/7539868 & (0) 83/5472091

Pharmacies

Khao Lak has many pharmacies, most in La On, but some also in Bang Niang. In the pharmacies, which are visited by both locals and tourists, you can seek advice on health and get most of the medications you also get in Europe – some with different names / packaging – and also several that require a prescription at home such as antibiotics against bladder infections. The pills are often not sold in the package, but in a small plastic sleeve where only the medication name and dosage will be written on. (e.g. 3x1/d). Package inserts are completely missing most of the time.

As in other pharmacies in Asian countries, it is also possible that you receive counterfeit drugs – and there can be just about anything in it. Although most pharmacies in Khao Lak look very neat, keep that in mind and take your regularly needed medications from home.

Traffic In Thailand: A Survival Guide

Driving in Thailand is like in an bumper car, only that you try NOT to hit anyone.

In Thailand you **drive on the left side of the road**, so the cars have the wheel on the right side. If you are not used to this perhaps you should apply a "keep left" sticker on the wheel – However, the biggest problem to remember this is on lonely roads ... which are rare in Thailand.

Expect everything, anytime: other drivers often behave erratically, are changing lanes without looking or indicating, run over red lights or stop on short notice, turn onto the road abruptly. At night many drive without any functioning light and on the wrong side of the road. Be attentive and ready to brake, especially at intersections and the entrance of side roads.

The emergency lane next to the road is often used by motorcycle and bicycle riders as well as these small, moving stalls that are simply too slow for the normal road, by cars to avoid a collision with other cars overtaking on the other side of the road, or if someone is waiting in the middle of the road to make a U-turn to the right.

There are **traffic lights** on some crossings in Thailand – on the way up north from the airport in Phuket there are two with a countdown, which show the seconds you have to wait until the next phase (green or red). At most traffic lights a left turn is permitted if the road is free ... even if the lights are red. Some Thais do even not stop at all or go early, if the light is red.

U-Turns: Down in Phuket they prefer U-Turns instead of traffic lights. The roads are often dual carriageways for longer distances with a green median strip in the middle that prevents you from crossing ... and if your turn off is on the other side, a U-turn (which are far apart) is the only possibility to get there. Be careful because people have to wait to make the turn (usually in the middle of the street), and some have no patience and simply go into the traffic. Fortunately this is not as common in Khao Lak.

Overtaking: Slower vehicles are passed by, even if it is not safe. This is done on the right or the left, and partly on the track of the oncoming traffic, which must dodge. So you always have to expect to see a car or van suddenly coming towards you in the same lane. It is a good idea to keep to the far left especially in front of hilltops.

Right of way: The same rules apply as in Europe ... many just do not stick to it. Especially bigger cars often take the right of way and where there are gaps, someone surely pushes in. You have to be equally unscrupulous or you will barely be able to enter into the traffic when turning.

For motorcyclists: **wear a helmet**. Yes – you will see a lot of (local) people not wearing a helmet, and it is hot, but ... this is not only an important protection for you, but also required by law. Even if the police are less interested in the tourists than in the locals, this is one of the things they check at the police stations and checkpoints and you can see many Thais suddenly bring out a helmet there. The same goes for **wearing the seat belt** in a car.

At **the police checkpoints** they check – outside of them the police is little interested in the traffic. Motorists are less checked than motorcyclists ... except for the dangerous days between Christmas and New Year and around Songkran when people are drinking and driving and the number of accidents and fatalities rise up – this time is also called "the 7 Days of Danger". Police check the driver's license, valid insurance, helmet, and seat belt.

Fines you have to pay immediately at the police station or the temporary cash stations. But with the receipt you are "immune" (for the same accusation) within the next 24 hours. This means you do not have to pay for the same thing again, even if you are still not wearing a helmet...

Drinking and driving: Thailand has a maximum blood alcohol limit of 0.5 mg (0.2 mg if you have not had your license for 5 years yet). Checks are seldom, but those caught are facing unpleasant consequences: prison in a mass cell and a bail of 20'000 baht to get out again. The final fine will be determined at court (between 2000 to 10'000 baht). And if you fall into the hands of a corrupt police officer this can get even more expensive.

Gas stations are not open 24 hours; most close after 8 pm. At the gas station you do not fill up yourself, but ask the staff. Simply tell them the desired mixture: Diesel 91 (Normal) or 95 (Super) and either "Full" or the amount for which you want to fill. You are told by the rental agency which one goes into the tank – or you can look it up on the tank lid.

Road maps: At the rental station you only get some very rough and undetailed tourist maps. I would still always ask what they have. You can buy a good "Road Map of South Thailand" in the 7-Eleven. On smartphones Google Maps helps greatly, as do some apps – Although the maps of Scout, which I have used successfully elsewhere, are still not detailed enough..

In Case Of A Traffic Accident

You occasionally hear horror stories of what could happen after an accident in Thailand. This is often based on the assumption that the tourist, no matter what happened, is guilty because: "If the tourist had not been there, then the accident would not have happened." That is no longer necessarily so, but it is always a good idea if you look for some Thai speaking help (for example from the rental agency or the Tourist Police) in order to clarify the matter.

Procedure:

Leave the vehicles how they are until the police arrive. (It may well be that the other participant of the accident flees from the accident scene – a photo of the car with number plate is helpful).

There are no warning triangles here ... a couple of tree branches put down on the road serve the same purpose. So be careful when you see this – though they often lie very close to the car.

Call the owner of your car (the rental agency) that will send a claims adjuster to you for the insurance.

Stay and wait quietly.

The rental agency usually provides a replacement car.

With motorcycles it must usually be negotiated on site who pays how much (due to lack of insurance) ... mostly you (and not the rental agency) have to pay. It is usually cheaper to have the repairs done yourself because the owner otherwise may demand his own (probably inflated) price for it.

Emergency numbers: **Firefighters 199**

Police 191 or 1155

Tourist Police 1699

Thai for Tourists

Because it is always good to know a few words of the local language – and this is well received. It is not a requirement, but it improves any contact ... and sometimes you receive a better price when negotiating. With English you get very far (especially in tourist places like Khao Lak and Phuket), but it is worth to learn some expressions:

Hello / Good day: sa-wade-krab (for men) / sa-wade-ka (for women)

Goodbye: La gon krab (for men) / la gon-ka (for women)

Yes: Chai-krab (for men) / Chai-ka (for women)

No: Mai Chai-krab (for men) / mai chai-ka (for women)

Thank you: Kop-kun-krab (for men) / kop-kun-ka (for women)

Please! Mai ben rai-krab (for men) / Mai ben rai –ka (for women)

What is the price?: Tau tai krab? (for men), Tau tai-ka? (women)

I: Phom (for men), Tschan (for women)

My name is: Phom tschü (for men) / Tschan Tschü (for women)

I want to go to: Phom bpai krab (men) / Tschü bpai ka (women)

Toilet?: Hong nam

Temple: Wat

Waterfall: Nahm Dtok

Island: Ko

Small road: Soi

Market: Dtalaad

Sea: Thalee

Space for your notes:

Printed in Great Britain
by Amazon